Carl Christian Thorwald Andersen

The chronological Collection of the Kings of Denmark

Carl Christian Thorwald Andersen

The chronological Collection of the Kings of Denmark

ISBN/EAN: 9783743339118

Manufactured in Europe, USA, Canada, Australia, Japa

Cover: Foto ©ninafisch / pixelio.de

Manufactured and distributed by brebook publishing software
(www.brebook.com)

Carl Christian Thorwald Andersen

The chronological Collection of the Kings of Denmark

CONTENTS.

I.

The time before and under Christian IV (the Renaissance). 1448—1648.

II.

From the introduction of absolutism to the French revolution (rococo style).

Introduction.

In the beginning of the year 1606 king Christian IV bought
a number of private gardens and grounds, situated close outside
the ramparts of Copenhagen between the northern and eastern
gate, in order to form of them a large garden with a ›Summer-
house‹, where he could seek repose, when he wished for a short
time to withdraw from the noise of the capital and nevertheless reside near it. Already in the third month of the named
year the work began, but, it is probable, it was not finished before
the year 1625, although the little palace — ›Rosenborg‹ it was
called — long before its completion was inhabited by King Christian.

Rosenborg is built. in the so-called German-Netherlands Re-
naissancestyle, which aimed at effecting a harmonious combination
of the Gothique and the Antique, by means of transferring the
principal forms of the gothic architecture: slender perforated turrets,
crenulated gables, pointed roofs, winding staircases &c., but, on
the other side, by seeking its types in the Antique, where the
question of mere ornamentation was concerned. As for the palace
itself it is built of red bricks and sandstone from Gulland; the latter
is employed ornamentally throughout: borders, window frames,
figures, points, flatbands and embellishments, which all contribute
to bring animation and variety to the great facades. The edifice
consists but of one main-building with three stories. Its principal
fronts have a length of 150 feet and turn towards west and east;
the west-side has a turret, 160 feet high, the east-side three: two
square turrets, 116 feet high, and in the middle an octogonal
turret, 65 feet high.

In the course of time Rosenborg has undergone many changes
in regard both to its exterior and to the entire embellishment of
its interior; but it was left to the improved artistic taste of the
latest time, with its affection for the monuments of the Past, to

redress the wrong. The restoration of the castle's exterior and interior has (1878) been upon the matter completed.

Until about the middle of the 18 Century at certain times of the year, namely spring and autumn, Rosenborg served as a residence for a series of Danish kings, of which the interior of the building itself contains many a witness in the different rooms and saloons, that in the course of time have been altered by the royal inhabitants and refurnished according to the varying taste of the periods. In passing through the personal appartments of these kings, we therefore meet not alone the Renaissance, but also the Rococo style in its different shades, as by degrees it developed itself.

Already in the time, when Rosenborg was a royal residence, it was used as a depository for dresses, weapons, ornaments and objects of art &c., that had belonged to the kings of Denmark after Christian IV. These objects were however during a long period collected and put aside without any critical selection, but simply to preserve them because they had belonged personally to the sovereigns. It was at the conclusion of the last and the beginning of the present century, that the thought first awoke of the historical significance, such a collection would receive from an intelligent arrangement and the separation of heterogeneous objects. The ever increasing interest for memorials of the past caused this thought to grow and gave birth from time to time to many attempts towards an adequate historical arrangement, which has at last resulted in the present Chronological Collection of the Kings of Denmark — a name the Rosenborg collection received by Royal resolution Dec. 28, 1858, with intent that it should form a depository of articles pertaining to modern times, so as to supplement, in some degree, the Museum of the Northern Antiquities and, as far as possible, with »Royalty« for central point, present a national, historical picture of modern cultivation, during the absolute monarchical period from 1660 to 1848.

That which has assisted in no small degree to forward this work — the honour of which is exclusively due to the present director of the Collection, Mr. J. J. A. Worsaae — has been partly the fact, as we have said before, of the successive changes, which the interior of the palace has undergone in the course of time, so that it has come to form a natural frame for the chronological arrangement of the objects, there by setting forth the characteristics of every period for more clearly; and partly the circumstances, that latterly, that is, from 1858, the historical material itself has been increased to a very great extent by the fire of Frederiksborg palace and the dissolution of the Art-Museum. A considerable space has also been gained for the arrangement of objects, that include those belonging to the last Century, during which Rosenborg has not been the residence of any king, and by the removal of the royal cabinet of coins and medallions, which was formerly located in the castle. By the arrangement of this space it became possible, which want of room had prohibited before, to present to view a very important period of culture, viz: the time before and after the great French revolution: the termination of the French Rococo-period (the Decadence), the Imperial Renaissance, and our own time.

After having thus in a few words explained the intention and plan of the collection, we shall only add, that it is not our purpose in this book to give a full account of every object, contained in the museum, but only to assist in retaining the impressions, which an attentive and careful survey of the collection has left in the mind after a single visit. Just as during a hasty visit to a large and varied museum it is best before all to fix the attention upon that which impresses the character of the whole on the mind, so it is our one sole aim, to recall to the memory of the reader his transit from room to room and to freshen the principal features of the outline of a great historical picture, on which we hope the visitor has dwelt with pleasure for a short time

In passing through the rooms the following 3 principal periodes must be well remembered as frames for the compartments of the picture: 1, the time before and under Christian IV; 2, the time from the introduction of Absolutism until the French revolution; 3, the time from the French revolution to the present day.

The time before and under Christian IV (the Renaissance). 1448—1648.

This period, which, as will be remembered, also seeks to be represented by the objects preserved in the last division of the Museum of Northern Antiquities, forms a natural introduction to the time of the Sovereignity properly so called. In it were collected, and encreased day by day, the materials that sooner or later must have led to an outbreak, in which the struggle between the regal and aristocratic power would be finally decided. It is therefore perfectly in order, that in a collection, whose object is the illustration of the history of the sovereign power (absolutism) should begin with the time, immediately preceding this; and it is fortunate, that in Rosenborg we find materials, exactly adapted to represent this antecedent period in a full, clear light. But the natural ground for this lies in the fact that the castle, raised by the great architect Christian IV in the flower of his age, continued ever afterwards to be his favorite residence and thus must unavoidably have come to acquire and retain many traces of this preference and of his occupations and manner of life within its walls.

The style of Christian IV — as we may justly call it because we do see himself and the influence of his rich, strong Character in his numerous Renaissance-buildings — is remarkable for a simplicity and taste, with strict attention in every respect to stability and use, which forms a striking contrast to the encumbered magnificence and show which appear in the declension of a later period of culture. We can obtain a good idea of this from what the interior of Rosenborg still retains from its earlier days in the rooms, which contain that division of time, with which we shall here first make acquaintance, namely 1) the Audience-chamber of Christian IV, 2, his Bedroom and 3, his Workroom (study).

A long corridor runs along the eastwall on the ground floor, into which the visitor enters by the small flight of stone steps, which lead from the north-east tower to the castle. This corridor, which connects the two saloons at the extremeties of the lowest part of the castle, has a beautiful gypsum roof, part of which is of the time of Christian IV, and a flagged pavement. A winding staircaise from the middle of the outermost wall leads through the centre tower up to the other two stories of the castle. The walls of the corridor are adorned with paintings; different pieces of furniture are likewise found here, the most striking of which are:

A table (of the time of Frederik II) with an oblong stone-slab, on which lines for a kind of game are incised.

A table with an artificial marble slab, the inlaying of which represents a map of Denmark in the time of Christian IV, in which Sleswick is designated by its ancient name Sonderjylland (»Süderjutland«, South-Jutland); the table is in all probability the work of a Dutch artist.

The oaken door of a closet is placed on the wall, on which the escutcheons of Denmark and Mecklenburg are richly carved. The upper part forms a projecting cornice, on which are two busts in metal of Frederik II and his queen.

Two portraits in reliévo of Frederik II in alabaster, and two busts of Charles I of England and of his queen, Henriette Marie. These busts, of which the first is of particoloured, the other of white marble, are the work of the renowned Italian Bernini.

Besides these there are the following paintings:

In the middle of the large wall hangs the genealogical-tree of Christian IV with 61 portraits (from his grand parents of the fourth degree).

In the southern and of the corridor:

Count Valdemar Christian. — Frederik III. — Ulrik Christian Gyldenløve and Hans Ulrik Gyldenløve (natural sons of Christian IV). — 3 portraits of Vilhelmine Ernestine (daughter of Frederik III). Christian »Albert« of Holstein-Gottorp and his wife Sofia Amalia — Christian V. — Rantzau. — Christian Bjelke. — Bishop Jesper Brochmand. — Lars Ulfeld. — Henrik Bjelke. — Ebbe Ulfeld. — Jens Bjelke (twice). — Gregers Krabbe. — Ove Bjelke. — Sigvard Grubbe. — Jørgen Bjelke. — Anders Sørensen Vedel. — Preben Gyldenstjerne. — Christian Rantzau. — Korfits Ulfeld. —

In the northern end of the corridor:

Otto Krumpen. — Peder Skram. — Birgitte Brockenhuus. — Holger Rosenkrants. — Erik Krabbe. — Hans Tavsen. — Ivar

Thott and his wife. — Niels Hemmingsen. — Birgitte Göye. — Frederik II. Albert Göye. — Johannes Friis. — Peder Oxe. — Henrik Rantzau. — Qveen Sofia. — Christian II. — Qveen Dorothea. — Niels Kaas. — Jørgen Rosenkrants. — Ludvig Munk. — Ellen Marsvin. — Princess Maria (married with Magnus, king of Livonia). Qveen Sophia as a joung girl. — Anne (daughter of Frederik II, consort of James I, king of England). — Christian IV and Qveen Anna Katharine (a full sized portrait). — The Electress Anna of Saxony (daughter of Christian III). — And finally: Christian III (a bust portrait engraved on a silver plate) and Ole Vorm (a bust portrait; copperplate, engraved by Haelveg). —

A Knights-banner of silk from the period of Christian IV, hangs over the genealogical-tree. It is divided into sqvares, red and yellow — the colours of the house of Oldenburg —. The monogram of Christian IV is in the centre, surrounded by the initial letters of his motto: R. F. P. (regnum firmat pietas) and the following device: NON IMPUNE ME LACESSES.

Over the northern door we see the Danish escutcheon as it was in the time of Christian IV, over the southern as it was after the introduction of Absolutism. The northern door leads into:

Christian IV's Presencechamber.

The walls in this saloon are of oak, divided by 22 richly carved oak pillars, between each of which on panels are inserted paintings (pastoral and hunting scenes), by dutch and flemish artists. The flat ceiling is in the same manner decorated by paintings on canvass and wood, and the floor is of marble. On the beautiful chimney-piece, that stands between the baywindows in the extreme northern wall, the date 1615 is inscribed. From the window in the eastern wall a speaking-tube runs for 150 feet through the wall; communicating with the saloon on the eastern side. In the southern wall of the saloon there are four closets, whose doors, when closed, correspond and make one with the decoration of the reste of the wall. Of the contents of these closets the following are most note worthy:

From the time of Christian I (1448—1481).

The Oldenborg horn.

This celebrated memorial of the past, which bears the usual form of a drinkinghorn of the middle ages, is of silver, richly decorated over the whole surface, partly with engraven figures of dragons and serpents, and partly with embossed or cast ornaments, which are fixed upon it, besides being in many parts enamelled. As regards the ornamentation the artist has evidently borrowed his motive from the German age of chivalry. The whole, one can suppose, has been intended to represent a burgh or walled town, the spires of which form the lid and knob, in which the points of the horn terminate, whilst the entrance is beneath the two towers by which, and two griffins with out spread wings, the horn is supported. There are also balconies, ladies playing on the lute, knights, esquires &c. — in short a picture in miniature of the life of chivalry is depicted in its many-coloured diversity. Of the inscriptions on the horn we must notice principally that which is twisted round the lid in monkish characters, to wit the names of the three kings: Baltazar, Jacpar, Melcior, which would seem to intimate that the horn had originally been intended for them. Upon the knob sits a little savage holding a narrow scroll, with the inscription: drinc al wt (Empty the horn!).

As regards the origin of the horn (of which however an old myth tells us, that in the year 989 it was presented to count Otto I of Oldenburg by a mountain nymph, who came out of the mountain Offenberg and approached him with it, when one day, having lost himself in the hunt, thirsty and discouraged he stopped his horse there) a very probable surmise is, that Christian I caused it to be made in 1474 by the sculptor Daniel Arctæus, who was called to Denmark from Westphalia. In this year Christian I had been invited by the German emperor Friedrich III and Charles the Bold, duke of Burgundy, to repair to Cologne for the purpose of mediating in the dispute, that had arisen between the archbishop and the chapter in that city. Cologne was the city of the Three kings, and the horn might have been intended as an offering to the guardian saints of the town, in case the mediation succeeded. This is strengthened both by the inscription before spoken of on the lid and other tokens. — The horn until the 17 Century was preserved in the castle of Oldenburg, but after the death of Anton Gynther it was brought to the artchamber of Copenhagen. —

A silver capsule containing a lock of hair of Christian I.

From the time of Christian II (1513—1523).

A gold ring in which a little uncut Sapphire is set. Round the circle is engraved: ave Maria gr. (gratiosissima). It belonged to the noble Elizabeth, the queen of Christian II, who received it from her husband on the day of their marriage, August 12, 1515.

Elizabeth was a daughter of Philip the Fair and sister to the emperor Charles V. Three years after the flight of king Christian from Denmark she died at a country-house near Ghent, in which town she is interred.

The handle of a knife in gold with the monogram of Christian II surmounted by a crown.

From the time of Frederik I (1523—1533).

A small swordblade with the pivot (the hilt is wanting).
Upon the flat side of the blade can be read: Fridrich I Konge y dannemarck og noric 1530 (Fr. I king of Denmark and Norway 1530).

From the time of Christian III (1533—1559).

A silver goblet with the arms of Denmark engraved on the side. It belonged to Christian III. — A little silver gilt time-piece with the hourplate on the obverse side and on which we further read the date 1557. It belonged to the queen of Christian III Dorothea, princess of Saxe-Lauenburg, who died 1571. — Queen Dorothea's bridal ornament ɔ: a gift from the queen to the town of Copenhagen. On a plate of silver gilt a wreath of foliage and flowers, also silver gilt, is seen, which surround the principal part: an eagle, which bears the Saxon escutcheon, with the date 1557, and upon its breast a large uncut sapphire. Over the eagle is set a clear emerald and sapphire and under it a saphire and amethyst, all of considerable size. The ornament also contains six large Norwegian pearls (there have evidently been many more).

As is wellknown, in those days the town hall of Copenhagen was the most fashionable place for festivals and assemblies in honor of the marriages of the daughters of the most respected and wealthy citizens. The gift was presented, that it might serve as the bridal ornament of every such bride upon her wedding day, and was for many generations held in time-honoured possession and preserved in the town hall, from whence it was brought some years ago to Rosenborg.

From the time of Frederik II (1559—1588).

The order of the elephant of Frederik II.

It is of gold, rather flat, and ornamented with enamel and other embellishments. On the one side, in a medallion, is a breast

portrait of the king in profile and under it in blue enamel the letters: M. H. Z. G. A. the kings motto: Meine Hoffnung Zu Gott Allein (my hope is in God alone). On the other side, also in a medallion, the letters F. S. interwoven (Fredericus Secundus) and underneath in blue enamel: T. I. W. B. the wellknown second motto of the king: Treu Ist Wild Brat (Wildbrat — his dog — is faithful). The order is suspended on a very finely finished long gold chain, to bear round the neck.

This example is of great interest from its being the oldest in existence. Of the order of the elephant see for the rest what is said under Christian V.

The order of the elephant of Frederik II.

The order of the garter of Frederik II.

This rare and valuable chain, which is about 2½ ells long, is formed of 26 round shields, knitted together by a sort of gold cord. The shields themselves are double red roses in enamel, surrounded by an interwoven blue enamelled band, on which is inscribed the device: »Honi. Soit. Qvi. Mal. Y. Pense.« Under the centre shield hangs the George and dragon in gold. On the ribbon for the knee is a gold clasp; it shows traces of enamel and is ornamented with rubies and diamonds. The ribbon is edged with white pearls, the device is written in rubies.

The English order of the garter is looked upon as the first European order. It was instituted by Edward III in 1350, but received new statutes under Henry VIII April 23, 1523. The dress of the order is an under-garment of white silke, interwoven with silwer, a cap and feather, and a blue velvet mantle, upon the left breast of which is placed an octagonal star with the cross of St. George and the ribbon with the device of the order. The

ribbon is borne under the left knee. The use of the chain dates first from 1522. — The example here spoken of was conferred on Frederik II with great pomp in the castle of Kronborg August 13, 1582.

There have been 7 Danish kings, who have received this order: 1, Erik of Pomerania. 2, Hans. 3, Frederik II. 4, Christian IV. 5, Christian V. 6, Frederik VI, and our present king, whose investiture took place in Amalienborg palace April 25, 1865.

A Gold ring with a blue Turquoise. Found in the coffin of Frederik II in the cathedral of Roskilde, when his corpse was examined in 1857.

A Toilet-glass in a silver gilt frame, adorned with garnets and amethysts; a great curiosity, which is also implied by the rich setting of the little glass. It belonged to Sophie (princess of Mecklenburg) the queen of Frederik II, who died 1631.

A very large glass-goblet (15 inches high and 5 inches in diameter) from which Frederik II once, in the year 1568, drank with many princes and noblemen, to see who could drink the most, of which the names and marks of the king and his fellow-champions, scratched upon the glass, are a witness.

Numerous plates, with disks of amber and borders of silver, on which are engraven two escutcheons. They came from Germany as a present to Frederik II.

A gold spoon engraved with the Danish arms.

A knife with an ebony handle on which are inlaid in silver the initial letters of the motto: M. II. z. G. a. and the date 1570.

A scepter in wood with inlaid ornaments of silver (scenes from the chase and similar subjects). It belonged to Frederik II. At the surprise of Kronborg by the Swedes it fell into the possession of Sweden, but was returned as a gift to Frederik VII.

Many weapons that have belonged to Frederik II, amongst others two swords with cross-hilts; the blades 1½ ells long. Two finely finished pistols with wheel-lock (the keys to which bear date 1585). Two fowling-pieces, the one of which is interesting from its having a little eye-glass fixed to the further and of the barrel, through which to take aim. Three hunting-knifes &c. &c.

From the time of Christian IV (1588—1648).

King Christian IV on the death of his father was scarcely 11 years old, for which reason the principal power during his minority lay in the hands of a regency. The **gifted boy** received an **excellent education, and** when in 1596 Christian himself assumed the **government of his** Kingdom, the young **ruler** winced a love of action and enterprise which promised well for his people. And he ended as he began; even as to the last he called forth and promoted arts, science and industry, and above all every undertaking favourable to the general welfare, so he was always ready to fight for his native land and to offer life and blood, when that was threatened. He conducted 2 campaigns against Sweden, the first 1611—1613 (the war of Kalmar), in which he was victor, and the second 1643—1645, in which he was unsuccessful. He engaged in the 30 years war (1618—1648), but again unsuccessfully, and in 1629 was forced to sign the peace of Lubeck. He had for queen Anna Catharina af Brandenburg, who died 1612. In 1615 he married with the left hand a young lady of the name of Kirsten Munk, from whom he separated in 1629 (K. Munk died 1658).

A time-piece. A spuare (two inches high, by four inches in length and breadth) silvergilt case **rests** upon lion's feet and is ornamented on all sides with **figures, flowers and lions,** in beautiful embossed work. The dial-plate **turns up, displaying** under its surface the following inscription **engraved in Roman characters:** »Anno 1584 **gaf** Konning Frederick **den Anden til Danemark och** Norge &c. **sin Sön** Kristian **dette Segeverk .** (In the year 1584 king Fr. II of Denmark and Norway &c. gave to his son Christian this time-piece.)

The coronation robes of Christian IV (August 29. 1596). They are in the style of a Spanish knight (as are most of the coronation robes of the Danish kings), and are both elegant and costly: cloth of gold, interwoven with flowers of silver and silk: the seams of the jerkin being edged with silver braid. The breeches have a rich trimming of silver lace.

The Mantle of the Order of the Garter of Christian IV.
- His blood-stained linen (shirt, collar, handkerchief and wristband), cap and velvet jerkin, which he wore in the seafight by Fehmern (July 1st 1644).

'Many weapons amongst which must be particularly noticed.
The sword, with which Christian IV conferred knighthood. The blade is a Toledo, the hilt, in all probability of Danish workmanship, is of gold. Its bar and pommel are ornamented with table-diamonds and fine delineation in gold on blue enamel.

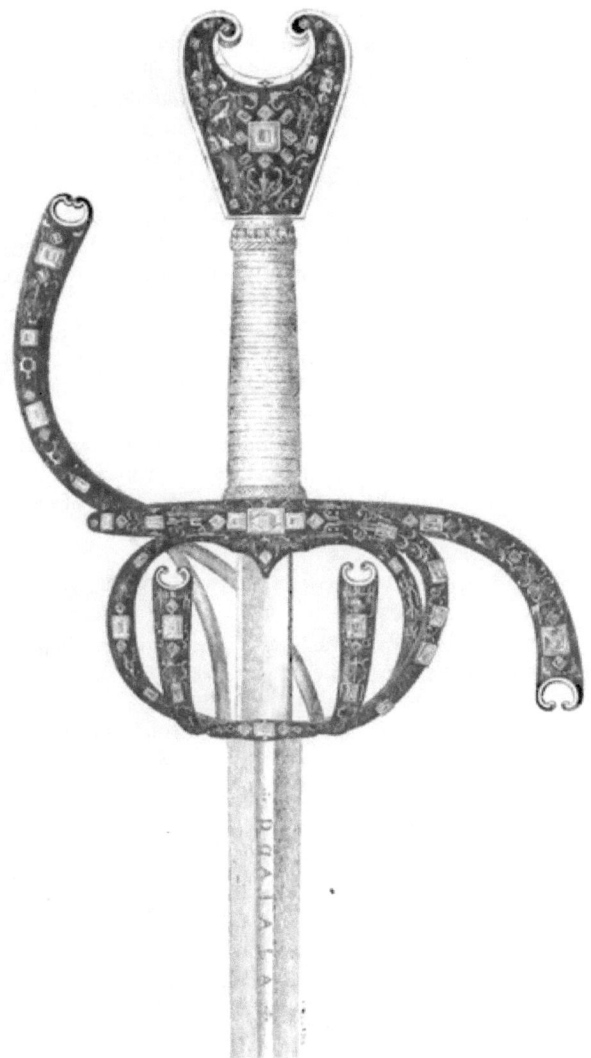

The sword, with which Christian IV conferred knighthood.

The mourning-sword he wore at the funeral of his eldest
son (November 1647). The hilt is of cut iron, and the blue blade
embellished with the arms of the Danish provinces. — ·

A sword with gold-plated iron hilt, bearing upon pommel the Danish escutcheon and the kings monogram in enamel.

A sword (of an admiral?) with gilded hilt and with a scabbard, which is covered with black velvet, and has a gilded mounting, that contains a little collection of instruments (a pair of compasses, knife &c.) of very beautiful workmanship. Upon one of them we see the date 1617.

A sword with a silvered iron hilt. On the blade is engraved: »Si deus pro nobis quis contra nos«. It belonged to Gustave Adolphus of Sweden, after whose death it was presented to Christian IV.

Three fowling-pieces with wheel-locks; the barrels are richly inlaid with ivory and mother of pearl; two of them were probably presented to Christian IV on his coronation by a foreign nobleman.

Lastly let us remark a cane with a silverbutton screwed on it, containing a compass and silver pointer, whilst the stick itself contains different instruments (the square, a pair of compasses, knife &c.).

Furthermore the closets contains the following note worthy objects:

A medallion in gold, which has probably belonged to an ancient insignia of the Order of the Garter. It is flat and two inches in diameter. On the front, in relief, upon an engraved and enamelled background, St. George appears on a white horse, doing battle with the dragon and surrounded by many animals. On the enamelled reverse Joseph and Mary kneel by the Holy child in the crib.

A splendid little gold piece: St. George standing by a white horse, with upraised sword in act of striking down the dragon. The whole adorned with enamel and a multitude of diamonds, large and small. On the sword are three small pearls. It is about three inches high.

A scent-box, one inch two l. high. By a chain, composed of small death's heads of coral and of goldbeads, hangs the principal object, which is a white enamelled death's-head of gold, having at the top a rim of small jewels and a stud, that takes off, when the box shall be opened. The head opens in two parts, the one contains a sponge, the other six small departments, each for its own perfume, the name of which is inscribed on the respective covers.

As regards the remaining objects in the presencechamber the most striking are:

In the centre of the floor:

An embossed and engraved cabinet of gilded metal, inlaid with ebony and resting upon four gilded metal lions. The leaf, which lets down, bears on the outside the date 1580, but even without this it would have been easy to assign to the furniture within a few years the date, at which it was mode. Its entire character (its constructive form, the many drawers, the delicate woodwork and engraved and embossed metal ornaments) clearly prove it an excellent specimen of the work of this kind, that was general towards the conclusion of the 16te century, and principally in Germany, from whence it certainly come.

On the cabinet stands a time-piece, that measures with the stand and figure on the top 1 ell 5 inches. The stand is of ebony, resting upon four shield-bearing lions. The upper part is formed of a sort of six-circled crown, that terminates at the top in a figure holding a halbert in the one hand. Under the curvatures, on a chair with the Brandenburg eagle behind it, sits a figure with a crown and sceptre, surrounded by 7 smaller figures.

In the north-east corner:

A clock. Made in Strasbourg by Isaac Habrecht, who in his day was renowned as a watchmaker and astronomer. With the wooden foot, upon which it stands, it is 4 ells high. It is very ingeniously constructed, indicating amongst other things the changes of the moon and year, and possessing musical-works, bell-chimes, twirling-figures, a crowing cock &c.; in imitation of the celebrated clock in the cathedral of Strasbourg.

In the north-west corner:

A vigorous and characteristically conceived metalbust of Christian IV in his latter days. We do not know what master produced this excellent work; the casting has been executed in Glückstadt.

The bedroom of Christian IV

lies in the north-east tower by the side of the audience-chamber. The upper portion of the walls is covered with green-watered gold flowered moire; the under is formed in panels, which are ornamented, amongst other designs, with one male and seven female portraits and pictures of the kings favorite hounds »Wildbrat and Tyrk«. The panels of the door contain a pair of

The bedroom of Christian IV

Venetian prospects. The ceiling has a rich decoration of gilded carving, which frames a painting — Medor and Angelika — and the floor is of Gothland flagstone. The fire-place is in the north-east corner.

The most striking objects here are:

In the closet:

The silvergilt compasses of Christian IV with date 1595. — His ship's hand-lantern of silver. — Two small lamps in the form of ships, with keels of rock-crystal. — A two-eared porcelain tankard, painted blue and white.

The cover bears a gilt plate, with an engraved inscription dated 1723, but the tankard itself was brought from East India in 1621 by Ove Gjedde.

A pair of scales, with bowls and weights in silver; used by Christian IV to weigh out gold and silver to the master of the mint. — Some of Christian IV's turning toils (Two flutes &c.). — Three goblets, of which the glass one with silver cover, on which his monogram is engraved, was used, according to tradition, as his favorite drinking vessel. Upon its sides the arms of the Danish provinces are cut. On the other two, which are silver (one gilded), the kings monogram appears; the ungilt silver one bears also an inscription, denoting, that the cup was made from money, which in the year 1600 the king had won from four courtiers in a mutual bet, which of them first should became intoxicated between the 6th of February and Easter in the preceding year.

— — — — — — — — —

Hov fyrst auff dem sig drucken drack
Fraa Blide Maanets den 6 Dag
Till Paask y thet fogangen Aar.

— — — — — — — — — —c

A double hourglass with a gold frame, upon which is the monogram of Christian IV and the date 1633 in enamel. A miniature model of Rosenborg executed in bone, as Christian IV first intended to construct it. — A small hand-mirror. The back, which is covered with black velvet, bears the monogram of Christian IV in enamelled gold, surrounded by one of his two mottos (Jehova dirige cor meum), also in enamel.

A chalice with consecrated — waferbox, paten and cup. All of the finest gold, ornamented with engraving, enamel and precious stones, amongst others two large rose diamonds, which form the eyes **of** a death's head upon the stem of the chalice. The whole weighs 155 ounces and belonged to the sister of Christian IV, Augusta, duchess **of** Holstein-Gottorp. The cup bears the date 1632. —

A chalice and paten (the chalice like the foregoing 9 inches high). It is an extraordinarely beautiful and artistical work, conjectured to have been executed in Holland. **Under** the convexity of the cup, and also upon the foot, a net of green, white and blue enamel is spread in twisted Arabesque, united into one whole by 66 enamelled rosettes, all in open work. Upon the paten likewise found enamelled ornaments. These magnificent pieces of workmanship, which weighs 87 ounces, are according to tradition a gift to Christian IV **from a** Dutch congregation in Denmark.

A large polygonal crystal **goblet** with crystal cover, ornamented with gold rims. —

An oval **agate** bowl, 9 inches high, relief outside and the date 1620. In the middle of the cover is an enamelled gold figure, that holds a shield with the arms of Wurtemberg, inclosed in a frame of diamonds; won by Christian IV in a tilt.

A goblet of lapislazuli of a rare **size**, and many smaller goblets of jasper, agate &c. **Two gold** goblets, the one with a cover and richly ornamented **with rubies, the other** with the name of Christian IV and **the date 1644. — Lastly we** find **in** the closet two miniatures **of** Christian **IV and Kirsten** Munk, painted 1623. —

Besides these two we find upon the walls **of the** bedroom a **great many other portraits: Christian IV** (8 pictures of different **size). — The same** (composed of small microscopic **letters).** — **The same (a copper** plate due **to** Haelweg, after the **picture of Carl v. Mandern).** — **The** same **upon** the bier (the **sketch of** J. G. Reinold is also here). — The **same,** outside **of a closed** tablet **from 1638; inside a** black tablet **(which has a** little indicative drawing — soap-bubbles and **an extinguished light** — and **an** inscription): **the king** used this **to set down in the evening** memoranda of **the most** important **things, he must attend to do** the next day. — **Lastly Christian IV as the negociator** of peace, painted wood **in** grey **on grey by** A. van der Wenne (who died 1650). This highly interesting allegorical picture represents the king with the princes Christian and Frederik with their consorts close to him; also the children, **then** living, by Kirsten Munk: count Valdemar Christian and the **ladies** Sophia Elisabeth, Leonora Kirstine, Elisabeth Augusta, Christiane and Hedevig; and lastly we see the foreign ambassadors at the Danish court &c. — Prince Christian (on horseback); the same (as a boy). — Prince Frederik (as a boy). — Leonora Kirstine (a portrait copied after the original in the possession of her descendant count Waldstein Wartemberg in Wienna).

On the walls we see further:

A painting representing the Derision of the Redeemer. Painted after a dream Christian IV had once in Rothenburg, of which we learn more from the declaration, drawn up in his own hand in German and laid in the frame.

Over the door: The antlers of a deer which on Dec. 8. 1611, being frightened by the Swedes, who were attempting to surprise the fortress of Kalmar, fled into the place, putting the Danish garrison on their guard.

In the windows: A box, bound with iron, a little handprinting press, and a stamp with the signature of Christian IV, intended for use upon busy days. — A brass chaffing-dish, marked with the date 1636 and the monogram of Christian IV and Elinore Kierstine . It has belonged to the outfit of El. Kirstine Ulfeld. —

On the floor:

A table of ebony. The disk rests upon four turned pillars and is ornamented with nine engraved round silver plates of different sizes, enclosed within a wreath of foliage of silver and mother of pearl. —

The 21st of February 1648 (old style) Christian IV caused himself to be brought from Frederiksborg to Rosenborg. His days were even then numbered, a week after he breathed his last in this little modest chamber, February 28th 1648 at 5 o'clock in the afternoon.

The Workroom of Christian IV.

Thus is the room designated, which was set apart by the monarch for his own particular use, during his residences at Rosenborg. It is separated directly from the Presencechamber, but has retained nothing unaltered of its original state, except the beautiful gypsum ceiling; the paintings in it are from a later period. The panels of the walls, that are green lackered and ornamented with Japanese figures in gold, date from the original architect, whilst the rest, painted in imitation of tortoise-shell, originate from Christian V. A fire-place of sandstone stands between the windows, which, newly restored, beam in gold and various colours, as in the first days of the castle. The beautiful marble floor is also a restoration of the present day.

We shall notice here:

A set of trappings for a horse. Saddle, housing and holsters of black velvet, upon which, as well as on the crupper, is an extraordinary rich decoration of pearls and gold embroidery; chased gold figures and enamelled clasps, rubies, sapphires and rose-diamonds. The pommels of the pistols are of gold, adorned with enamel and precious stones. —

These costly trappings were after tradition a present from Christian IV to his son prince Christian, the king-elect, on the occasion of his marriage with Magdalene Sybille, that took place in Copenhagen October 5th 1634. On this occasion a magnificence and festivity was displayed, such scarcely ever had been heard of before, and which continued for many days. One of the most splendid banquets was held in Rosenborg October the 9th. We have no certainty as to where this work was produced; but there is not the slightest doubt that it is Danish, since at this very time we have better goldsmiths work known to have been produced by native artists.

A series of dresses, worn by Christian IV, of brocade, cloth of gold, Brabant cloth and silver-moire. We would especially distinguish a most costly and elegant dress with jerkin, trousers and mantle of gold moire, interwoven with bouquets of silver-flowers.

A rich mourning-dress of black Brabant lace, worn by Christian IV at the funeral of his son prince Christian (Nov 1647).

The dresses here shown are in the style of the Spanish-Netherlands, which universally prevailed during the first fifty years of the 17th century, the characteristics of which are to be sought, partly in the materials (brocade, silver moire &c.), partly in the mantle, the unusually short waist, long skirt, broad embroidered linen collar (Dan: Christian IV's cravat, Engl: Vandyke-collar) and wide top-boots.

A fountain, which belonged to queen Anna Kathrine.

It stands upon a table of ebony edged with silver and supported by three silverpillars, which again rise from a triangular ebony foot, that finally rests upon three knobs of the same wood. The fountain proper is of silver. It has two reservoirs — an upper one for incense, a lower for perfumed water, — which are supported by three octogonal hollow pillars with taps in the middle.

The fountain of queen Anna Kathrine.

At the foot of the pillars are three silver dishes to receive the water, that flows when the taps are opened. Between the pillars rest a beautifully executed group of Actæon and Diana with three nymphs &c. The whole, including the table, is about 3 ells in hight.

A looking-glass in an ebony frame, decorated with two small portraits of Christian IV and Anna Kathrine, many allegorical figures and numerous ornaments, all in silver and, like the woodwork itself, excellently executed in the style of the renaissance.

This mirror, together with the fountain and the ebony table spoken of before in the bedroom, have in all probability formed parts of a complete and large set of furniture, which belonged to queen Anna Kathrine. It dates from about 1610.

The writingtable of Christian IV, of polished wood, resting upon four turned legs, and enclosed with a lid. Under this is a writingslab, covered with green velvet, and many spaces, in which are ink-stands and sandboxes of polished metal.

A cabinet of ebony, decorated outside with tortoise-shell and ivory, inside on the door by paintings &c. The underpart is a black lackered table upon four turned legs, and has a leaf, that draws out for use as a writing-table.

A pedigree upon parchment. It dates from 1636 and shows the connection between the Danish royal house and the princely family of Sleswick-Holstein-Gottorp.

A calendar, painted on wood, called: »Calendarium aureum«, with many golden rules for our wellbeing in this world &c. It is the work of one of Tycho Brahes disciples, Petrus Fischer.

A portrait of Christian IV, embroidered in silk, executed under Frederik III by an embroider in pearls, Clas Harder.

Further still 3 portraits of Christian IV.

1, as young man, by van Doort; 2, on horse-back speaking about the fortification of Copenhagen with engineer Stenvinkel; 3, as an old man; and

Portrait of Prince Christian and of his wife Magdalene Sybille. —

A drinkingcup, that represents Christian IV as tilting at the ring.

It is composed of an eqvestrian statue of the king, 28 inches high. He is clad in armour, wearing on his head a hat and feather, a tiltingbar in his hand, with which he has taken down the ring, that hangs between two columns, 28 inches high. Under the horse there is a figure dancing, supposed to represent the kings court jester. When used as a goblet, a mark upon the neck of the horse indicates the point where the head, which forms the lid, separates from the body. Upon the columns are incised the names and escutcheons of many princes and knights.

These names and escutcheons seem to denote the occasion, for which this costly object (which weighs about 1000 ounces) was furnished, being those of the most skilful knights at the great games of chivalry, held on the Amager-sqvare in Copenhagen the 3rd and 4th of September 1596 in honour of Christian IV's coronation. The king himself shone as victor on that occasion; in 340 tilts he took the ring 206 times. He never lost his affection for all knightly conduct and department In the year 1634 he again threw into the shade all his competitors in the chivalric sports held in honour of the marriage of his son. Not less significant of him in this respect is the injunction he gave his nobles on that occasion to exercise themselves well in dancing, so that they could appear with befitting decorum at the festivals.

An ivory relievo: Apollo's revenge upon Marzyas and Midas. The figures are very raised and almost round. The work is executed after the design of an Italian master and was finished in the year 1624.

Over the doors:

Eight Chinese figures in porcelain, brought home by Ove Gjedde.

In the glass-case by the one window is noticeable:

The cover of a genealogical album of gold, with flowers, birds, the escutcheons of Denmark and Holstein, the date 1613 &c. in enamel. This tasteful work, a gem from the art of that time, belonged to Augusta, the sister of Christian IV, who married Johan Adolph of Holstein Gottorp.

A note-book with rich enamelled gold binding. It contains some french verses in the handwriting of Anna Kathrine, the eldest daughter of Christian IV and Kirsten Munk; she languished and died of sorrow about six months after her betrothed husband, the lord high steward Franz Rantzau, perished by an unlucky accident in the moat by Rosenborg (1632).

Four bracelets, that belonged to queen Anna Kathrine:

1, A gold chain bracelet; on every link the monogram of Christian IV is engraved, ornamented besides with enamel, rubies and table diamonds. 2, A pair of ditto: every other link shows the changing seasons in exceedingly beautiful embossed work, the alternate links enamelled and richly set with diamonds. 3, A bracelet with inlaid, plaited hair (Christian IV's), gold flowers, figures in enamel, diamonds and the initials A. C.

A sapphire one inch square, of a rare lucidity, probably used as a broach by Christian IV.

Two gold finger-rings in each of which is set a good sized sapphire, the one being engraved the monogram of Christian IV.

A medicine spoon. The spoon itself is a sapphire very clear and pure 1¼ of an inch in diameter. The shaft, which is about three inches long, is of embossed gold, enamelled and ornamented at the end with the initials C and K intertwined. It is a little chef d'oeuvre of goldsmiths work, and a present from Christian IV to Kirsten Munk.

A gold tablespoon with the monogram of Christian IV and the date 1632; another with a handle of coral and bowl of gold.

A watch in a case of rock-crystal; belonged to Christian IV.

A George and dragon (with gold chain to suspend it round the neck). It consists of a blue enamelled wreath and the device of the order, within which, in open work, is St. George slaying the dragon.

The Garter of Christian IV's Order of the Garter. With the device in rubies and ornamented with pearls. The buckle of enamelled gold, ornamented with rubies and diamonds.

The great seal of the kingdom. It is of silver; on the clasp, which formes the handle, is the date.

A silver signet in the form of a stamp. On the plate a crowned heart with a latin legend and the motto of Christian IV.

Numerous ornaments, that have belonged to Anna Kathrine, of pearls and gold, embellished with precious stones and enamel: A Cupid with bent bow, a bird, two lions &c.

A wreath formed of the 14 Danish escutcheons in enamelled gold, the topmost shield being the escutcheon of the whole kingdom.

An enamelled bust of Gustaf Adolph king of Sweden. supposed be a decoration, to wich the thirty years war gave rise.

Several cameos: portrait of Philip II of Spain &c.

Many examples of an order of knighthood — the armed hand. The badge of the order was a blue enamelled arm, ornamented with the monogram of Christian IV, that holds a naked sword in the hand. It hangs in a broad blue ribbon, by which the insignia is bound round the neck. Its original form was however soon

changed by its being joined to the order of the elephant. One
of the examples preserved here, which was the one borne by
Christian IV himself and which bears upon the elephant the date
1617, shows us the order in its changed form. The rest of the
examples were borne by the king-elect prince Christian.

The order of »the armed hand«.　　　　　Christian IV's order of the elephant.

The order was conferred for the first time in Kolding Dec. 2nd
1616 during the festivities on the occasion of the enfeoffment of
Sleswick to duke Friederich III, the nephew of Christian IV. This
solemnity was not however the cause of its institution, since it was
in realty instituted as a reward for valour three years before at
the conclusion of the war of Calmar. The names of the first
twelve knights have been preserved in old verse:

Fries, Lung, Scheel, Ranzou, Rantzou tu Bildeque, Rantzou,
Senekler, Sparr & Pens, Sandberg, Scheel, partis eqvestris.

The order however was only conferred during the time between
1616—1634.

Lastly we should here remark the different miniatures (17
in number) of Christian IV (13); queen Anna Kathrine; her brother
the Elector Johannes Sigismund; Magdalene Sybille &c. Many
of them are beautiful executed.

Two small busts (in relievo) in coloured wax of Christian IV in advanced age, the one executed in his last year. It represents the king in an admirals dress; from a gold chain round his neck hangs the speaking trumpet, through which he gave his orders on board. Both busts are the work of excellent, but unfortunately unknown masters.

If we now collect all the impressions, received during our visit to Christian IV's rooms, they will produce for us a full and complete picture of him and his time. We have been reminded, now by this and now by that object, of his numberless great qualities, his love of activity, his watchful attention, his bravery, his chivalry, his feeling for art and its productions &c., as well also of the faults, that clung to him, but which assuredly for greater part must be attributed to the age, in which he lived. But what above all will then most distinctly stand before us, is the strong impress of the clear and decided character everything here bears, so that it is with reason, that we designate the time, which in Denmark ended its course with king Christian IV, as a distinct period of culture which then reached its essential close.

Frederik III.

From the introduction of absolutism to the French revolution (rococo style).

The time of Frederik III (1648—1670).

On the death of Christian IV the throne stood vacant during many months, and Frederik III was chosen king only after having signed a deed, dictated by the late kings powerful son in law Korfits Ulfeld, the husband of Leonora Kirstine, by which the power of the nobility was increased to such a degree, that the regal power became a shadow for the benefit of a single privileged class. After the unfortunate war with Sweden, that ended in the peace of Copenhagen (May 27th 1660) in which the king and his gifted, but withal haughty and ambitious, queen Sophia Amalia (daughter of George duke of Brunswick Lyneburg and who died 1685) had won great popularity by their bold and patriotic conduct during the siege of Copenhagen, they succeeded by the assistance of the other orders of people, who were disaffected towards the aristocratic power, in changing the form of government: the royal power was made hereditary and absolute, and on the 18th of Oct. 1660 the oath of fealty took place before the exchange in Copenhagen.

This revolution thus introduces a new period into Denmark: from this time the royal power was the sun, around which politics, art, industry, all turned, in other words: the history of the monarch was in a wider sense the history of the land. But added to this, the era in our native country was contemporaneous with the great European tide of progress, which we can say lifted a peculiar age out of its billows, reforming everything, bringing new manners, new customs, new views — in a word: a peculiar period of culture, widely differing from the preceding one, came in with the advent of Louis XIV.

And most fortunate is it, that the collection of Rosenborg should just date from this time and from a king, who, himself a cultivator of the arts and sciences, had an eye to the significant importance of handing down from generation to generation the characteristic productions of every age. We shall find frequent occasion during our progress through this long and significant period to rejoice over the rich contributions, the collection offers for its comprehension.

The articles from the time of Frederik III are found in the Garden cabinet, the dark chamber and the so called marble chamber.

The Garden Cabinet

is the lowest apartment in the western tower of the castle. Its walls are covered with green, white and red watered silk, and the floor planched with a beautiful inlaying of oak and walnut wood; the chimney piece is of greenish marble, and the roof decorated by a large mythological painting, surrounded by a broad white border in stucco. This last is interesting because it leads us at once into the Rococo style under its first appearance amongst us; in spite of its richness of composition it in no degree excites the impression of overloading.

We have in the furniture here an extensive contribution in this direction. We will notice principally:

A table and a pair of candle stands. They are beautifully carved and ornamented with gilding and colour; the slabs of the gueridons are of scagliola, in which the arms of Denmark and Lyneburg are found; they belonged to queen Sophia Amalia.

We see by the closed crown, that is found here and there, among the other decorations upon the last named articles, that they date from 1660. Before this time the open crown was principally used; on the contrary the crown with the closed pillars bearing the globe and the cross on the top (te sign of the power by the grace of God granted to the kingdom) first came into use with absolutism.

Upon the walls are found:

Five portraits of Frederik III in different sizes (3 painted, one mother of pearl on ebony, one coloured wax). — Three portraits of queen Sophia Amalia (2 large, as a young woman, the other as when older — the last most probably by A. Wuchter - and a small one by Wolfgang Haimbach, representing the queen in the dress of a peasant girl as she appeared in a ballet). —

4 small portraits of the children of Frederik III. — Christian V in a very early age (upon a silverplate covered with gold varnish). — A large painting: Taking the oath of fealty before the exchange in Copenhagen, by Wolfgang Haimbach, interesting as a picture of the times. Over and by the side of this hang the portraits of the six men, who were the most influential in the introduction of absolutism: Hannibal Sehested, Schack, Nansen, Svane, Gabel and Henrik Bjelke. — 4 portraits of Anton Gynther

A table from the time of queen Sophia Amalia.

(2 painted, 1 embroidered in silk, 1 composed of small letters· 2 of his wife Sophia Kathrine. — Portrait of the horse »Cranich (a gift from Anton Gynther to Frederik III; its mane reached to the ground and the length of its tail was three times its height). — Portrait of Charles I of England, embroidered in silk. — A representation of the storm in Copenhagen the night between the 10th and 11th of February 1659. — The procession through the town after the oath of fealty. — And lastly, to be remarked as an interesting addition to the characteristics of Frederik III, a por-

trait of a resident clergyman in Bremen, on wood, painted by Frederik III whilst he was archbishop there.

Of the rest, that the room contains, we will notice:

Before the fire place:

The coat of arms of Frederik III as archbishop of Bremen. A mosaic of marble enclosed in a wreath of laurels, carved in gilded wood.

To the right upon the wall:

Two suits, embroidered in silver and gold, the one of which was worn by Frederik III the day on which he received the oaths of fealty. — A staff, the handle of which was a poleaxe made of the well known alchemist Borro's gold.

A candle stand.

Joseph Frants Borro, born in Milan 1625. After having roamed from land to land and led a life romantic and adventurous in the highest degree, now the all powerful favorite of a prince, now condemned and burnt in effigie, came in the autumn 1667 to Denmark, brought hither by that renowned scholar Ole Borch, whom he had succeded in completely winning over. The learned Frederik III, who, like so many other potentates of that time, favoured alchemy, received him royally and sometimes took part himself in his alchemical studies. At first Borro worked in the laboratory in Rosenborg garden, then he got a laboratory of his own behind the exchange, which in 1669 he removed to Østerport (the gold-house). On the death of the king his role was played out here; he left Denmark and finished his inquiet days as a prisoner in the castle of St. Angelus in Rome.

A herold's sword, fabricated in the Broby works in Funen 1648. Upon the blade the arms of the Danish provinces are engraved. The hilt is of gilded iron, the pommel of black velvet.

Broby manufactury of arms, established by some gentlemen of Funen and the marshal of the kingdom Anders Bille of Damsbo (who fell at Fredericia 1657), was destroyed by the Swedes and was never reestablished.

By the window to the right:

A mourning sword, worn by Frederik III at the funeral of his father. The blad is engraved, the hilt black iron. — A sword with gold hilt and gold-mounted scabbard and belt, likewise worn by Frederik III. — A sceptre of silver with the monogram of Frederik III. — A brace of pistols; the barrels inlaid with golden ornaments, the butt-ends with enamel and Bohemian

A Jewelbox.

stones. – A breech-loading rifle of 30 shots. — Two rifles with butt-ends inlaid with ivory and the Danish arms in enamelled gold. — A pair of gold mounted enamelled spurs &c.

In the glass-case to the left:

A Jewelbox of silver. The cover and sides are rendered transparent by 15 cut crystals, through which we see on the bottom of the box the judgement of Paris in embossed work. Around the crystals 62 large garnets are set, and these again are enclosed in a rich embellishment of flowers, leaves &c., the splendour of which is enhanced by a countless number of small diamonds. The casket, which is 18 inches long (beneath) and 12 inches high, was a present to Sophia Amalia from her daughter in law Anne, queen of England.

Two smaller jewelcases of agate with enamel and precious stones. — Two others of ivory.

A crystal goblet. The cup, 5 inches long and 3 inches high, is in the shape of a shell and externally has 8 heads cut in relievo. It rests upon the back of a figure bending forward, and bears on the base of the shell a winged genius. The stem is oval, and in front shews, in relief, the arms of Hesse, behind the motto of the landgrave Charles (candide et constanter) round a crowned shield. This extremely precious work of art is possibly a present from the aboved named prince, whose sister Charlotta Amalia was married to the crownprince of Denmark.

Many other articles of crystal, including a bowl, with incised designs, which rests upon a foot and is in the form of a ship.

A set (32) of chess formed of slate, the greater part of which are portrait figures (the kings Frederik III and Carl Gustaf; the queens Sophia Amalia and Hedewig Eleonora &c. &c.).

An elephant crushing an ibex with his trunk. It is an allusion to the defeat of the Swedish General Stenbock by Nyborg (Stenbock ɔ: ibex).

A round glass goblet with a cover, 9 inches high, decorated with ground ornaments; on the lid Frederik IIl on horseback; round the glass the battle in the Sound, the descent on Amager and the battle of Nyborg are represented. Below the following verse:

Dies ist der König Friederich,
Den Gott geführet wunderlich
Und Kopenhagen, Seine Stadt,
Die er im Sturm be Schützet hat.
Als Holland erst im Sundt gesieget
Und so der Schweden floth bekrieget;
In fühnen blieb ihr Stolzes Heer
Wie pharao Im Rothem merr.

A series of objects, rare by reason both of material and workmanship, the stones (topaz, onyx, aquamarina &c.), many of which are of an extraordinary size, in connection with the cutting and enamelling have produced little masterpieces of the jewellers art; remark for example the altar, the ornament with the aquamarina (the history of the Passion), and the topaz goblet.

A crystal goblet.

Remark also the beautiful tankard in amber with setting and foot of gilded silver.

Three gold goblets with green enamelled medallions, in which are the monogram of Frederik III and the escutcheon of Holstein; they belonged to the duke Frederik III, cousin to the king Frederik III.

A gilded silver chalice and paten bearing the monogram of Frederik III; used by the king, when he received communion.

A small round silverbox with the monogram of Frederik III in the bottom (used by the king as a pocket-box, to hold pomade for his beard).

In the open cupboard to the left:

At the bottom a small eqvestrian statue of Frederik III as a tilter, with pillars of silver, most delicately executed. Four larges and six smaller silver goblets in embossed work. — A silver globe, gilded and engraved, with the stand 21 inches high. — An ivory cup, 10 inches high, with three gold enamelled band; on the cover in enamelled gold a figure, representing a Greenlander, with a bow around his neck. — Many cups and goblets, formed from the horn of the Narwhal and Rhinoceros.

(It is most probable, that the greater part of these objects have been won in the games of chivalry; and indeed the inscriptions on some of them would seem to intimate as much.)

A silver goblet with a lid, 9½ inches high, called the Bornholm goblet.

According to tradition the first time this island was visited by Frederik III after the peace of Copenhagen, he drank from this cup with the chief men of Bornholm, who liberated the island from the Swedes. In the peace of Roskilde it had been ceded to Sweden, but the men of Bornholm, having won back their independence by their own exertions, on Jan. 8th 1659 transferred their allegiance by a deed of gift to the crown as a perpetual inheritance and possession. The leaders in the rising were the nobleman Jens Pedersen Kofod, the yeoman Niels Gummeløv and the clergyman Poul Anker.

Upon the wall:

Four oval silverplates and one, set in a frame, with embossed figures, in work so raised, as sometimes to be almost round.

In the glass-case upon the table:

A series of small portraits (36 in number) from which we distinguish the following: Frederik III enamelled upon a gold plate by

A. Prieur (1663), an excellent work; portrait of five of Frederik III's children, enamelled upon one plate by the same artist (1671); two in black slate plates (5 inches high and 4 inches broad) full length portraits of Frederik III and Sophia Amalia, inlaid in mother of pearl; enamelled miniature portraits of the two English kings Charles I and II, of queen Christina of Sweden, Carl Gustaf and his queen &c.

A round silver box containing a small piece of gold, fabricated according to tradition by Frederik III (Borro). — The favorite spoons and forks of gold of Frederik III and his queen. — Knives, forks and spoons with handles of agate, crystal &c.

An eye-glass of gold with case of the same metal. — A small collection of ornaments, in which pearls of peculiar forms are used as motive figures (fishes, mermaids &c.). — Signets of carved stones (chalcedony, topaz etc.) with enamelled handles; rings &c. — A collection of goldcups (13 in number), that fit one into the other; the exterior one is ornamented with four enamelled medallions, in each of which — also in enamel — is placed the escutcheon of Denmark and Norway, the three crowns, and the monogram of Frederik III.

The dark chamber

lies south of Christian IV's workroom. All the light, that it receives, comes from the window of the winding-stairs in the west-tower and from a little side-room, for which reason it is but little adapted for a museum. It was originally designed to serve as a bedroom. The ceiling is of white stucco, the walls covered with red damask and white silk. The marble floor is a restoration of the present day. Over the marble chimney-piece is a large Venetian mirror, set in a richly gilded frame in the elder rococo style.

In this room let us remark:

A bust of Frederik III in gypsum. — One of Griffenfeld, also in gypsum. The portrait of Frederik III on a dark embossed metalplate. — A half length portrait of Frederik III. It is of wax placed in a glass-case with the crowned monogram of the king; he is attired in a sort of Roman costume; natural size (artistically worthless). — Queen Sophia Amalia. A pendant to the one last named. — The portrait of the artist Jakob Hollænder (Dutchman). Holding one of his works in his hand, a carved ivory mug, which is deposited in the marble chamber. — Portrait of Jörgen painter.

An ebony cabinet, on the doors and drawers of which is
a rich covering, of curious design, in tortoiseshell, and it is further
decorated with gilded metal ornaments, inlaid with ivory &c.

An ebony cabinet with border of ivory. — Two tables
with slabs of scagliola; they have belonged to queen Sophia Amalia,
as proof of which her monogram and the arms of her family are
found in the inlaying.

The marble chamber.

that lies south of the last named room and the windows of which
look out upon the drilling-ground, dates from the time of Christian V
and furnishes a highly interesting example of the Rococo of Louis
XIV's days. Its walls and floor give name to the room, the
former being covered with marble coloured stucco, and the latter
having a chequered mosaic pavement of dark and light marble.
Burnished pilastres with Corinthian capitals break the flat surface
of the marbled walls, which are further decorated on the long
sides by eight round compartments, painted with the arms of the
Scandinavian kingdoms. On the doors we find the monograms
of Christian V and his queen. That which will principally strike
the visitor is the remarkable stucco-ceiling, whose alto-relievo (genii,
fruits, wreaths &c.), which encircles a multitude of painted compartments, containing representations of the arms of the Danish
provinces and many other subjects, cannot fail to give the highest
idea of the skill and boldness of the masters, who have produced it.

We find here from the time of Frederik III:

In the closets on both sides of the north door: Many dresses.

We would call particular attention to the one of dark brown
cloth; its cut is after the fashion of the Netherlands; down all the
seams and upon the front of the sleeves runs a rich trimming of
gold and silver lace. — As will be seen in the costumes from the
time of Frederik III the frock-coat forms one with the original
dress, and the cape (see the dress of Christian IV), which was of
Spanish origin, dissappears.

A hat bordered with broad gold galloon. — A sceptre of
the horn of the Narhwal; the ball and the ring of the ferule
are of enamelled gold and set with rubies. — A cane with a gold
top, enamelled with the three crowns, the monogram of Frederik III
and his motto: dominus providebit, and also with the inscription: Chacun a son Tour 1660, which has reference to the

The marble chamber.

moment, when by the introduction of absolutism the nobility had to bend at last to the royal power. — A hunting-sword; the hilt of horn bound with gold and ornamented with enamel and embossed gold lions. On the sword-belt are the initials of queen Sophia Amalia. — The gun of the same queen, with an ivory medallion inlaid in the butt end, bearing the initials S. A. and the motto of the queen: en dieu mon Esperance .

A great many articles of ivory, turned and carved: portraits in relievo, cups, boxes, drinking-horns &c., amongst which not a few even apparently insignificant things are of considerable artistic value, whilst others, besides the merit of skilful workmanship, desire great value from excellency of material and rare size.

Many of these works are certainly executed abroad (Augsburg and other places), but just as it is known that one article (a round box) was turned by Frederik III himself, so we also know that at the period under review not only foreign but also native artists distinguished themselves by the production of works of this kind in the land. Amongst the latter we would recall the memory of the celebrated artist Jakob Jensen Normand (born in Norway, died under Christian V as curator of the art-chamber and armourer), who, amongst other means, won himself a name by his carvings in sycamore and in the ivory of the narwhval and elephant. Amongst his works, here preserved, we will draw particular attention to the ships and boats, placed in the windows, and especially to the admirably finished model of the Norwegian lion a 44 gun frigate of the time of Frederik III.

Lastly let us remark a quantity of furniture of the time of Frederik III:

A large table, the slab of which is formed of the elder Florentine mosaic. — An ebony cabinet, the drawers of which are covered outside with dendrites. — A table with a scagliola slab. — A very beautiful cabinet for jewels; the drawers are lined with green velvet and covered outside with Florentine mosaics &c.

The Florentine mosaic as is well known is formed of hard stones (marble of diversified colours and shades) by the skilful arrangement of which pictorial designs are produced. The Roman mosaic on the contrary results from the employment of small squares of an artificial vitrious-substance. — Dendrit is a chalk-stone containing the appearance of trees in the stone, produced by the water pressing through the porous parts and depositing the decomposed particles, it has carried along with it, in different

forms as trees, shrubs &c. - Scagliola is a production of pulverized
and coloured alabaster from which pictures somewhat resembling
mosaic can be produced.

Frederik III died Febr. 9th 1670 having filled the throne for
22 years.

From the time of Christian V (1670—1699).

Christian V was the first Danish king, who ascended the
throne without subscription to the charter, dictated by the nobility,
and in the strength of his hereditary right. As prince he had
travelled abroad (from 1662—1663) and in the court of Louis XIV
had become acquainted with the pomp and magnificence, which
now as far as in him lay he sought to imitate in his own court.
He therefore amongst other innovations instituted a new order
of nobility, counts and barons (May 25th 1671), issued the first
ordinance respecting precedence, and renewed the order of the
Elephant and the Dannebrog (the white ribbon). From 1675—1679
he was engaged in the so called Scanian war with Sweden, in
which Niels Juel won his renown (battle in Kjøge bay, July 1st
1677 &c.). — Peter Griffenfeld, whose name was Schumacher
before he was ennobled, who in the first years of Christian V had
risen from honour to honour and won renown both at home and
abroad as Denmarks first statesman, during this war was deprived
of power and confined as a prisoner of state upon Munkholmen
(Norway). — In 1683 Christian V promulgated his Danish code
and 1687 his code for Norway. — Christian V was married with
Charlotte Amalia, princesse of Hesse Cassel (died 1714).

The articles of the time of Christian V are preserved in the
marble chamber, the south end-saloon (formerly called the Red
Apartment), the tower-room adjacent and the Rose upon the
first floor.

The marble chamber,

which has been described before, and, as we have said, was arranged and furnished under Christian V, gives indeed in itself a
good presentation of the taste of this king, and of his age, for
splendour and magnificence.

We find here some furniture of Christian V's time, from which
we will call attention to three cabinets; the first is of ebony with

Christian V.

an inlaying of tortoiseshell, interiorly; the second of walnut with
inlaid mosaic, and the third wholly covered with tortoiseshell and
exceedingly rich and tastefully ornamented with fillets and engraved arabesques in silver.

The last mentioned piece belongs to a kind of work, that
was brought into fashion under Louis XIV by the renowned wood-
carver André Charles Boule, from whom it took its name. He
was the first, who discovered how to inlay engraved silver ornaments in tortoiseshell.

Further we should notice two ivory caskets for jewels, the
larger ornamented with inlaid mosaics, the smaller with pictures
in a sort of silkembroidery, that is glued upon the exterior of
the sides and drawers.

The south end-saloon

answers to the audience-chamber of Christian IV at the opposite
end of the ground floor. It is tapestried with well preserved
hautelisse-tapestry of a bright red coloured ground, on which account in the time of Christian V it was called the Red Apartment«. It was used as a dining-room by Christian V, which is
apparently indicated by the richly painted decorations on the
ceiling (a band of musicians playing, dancing genii &c.), but at
all events we are reminded of this by the two immence »plate-
warmers before the fire-place, the beautifully made and engraved
dishes with silver stands belonging to them. The floor of white
marble has newly been restored. The chimney-piece of marble,
that stands on the south wall between the bay-windows, is also a
restoration of the present day. Above the chimney-piece in a
richly finished marble frame we see a portrait of Christian V.

The hautelisse tapestry of this saloon was woven in Kjøge
probably after the designs of the painter Bendix Grotschilling the
younger (born 1655, died as the curator of the art-chamber 1707).
The distinction between basselisse and hautelisse tapestry depends
on the warp lying horizontally or vertically. This fabric originated
in France, for which reason it is frequently denominated Gobelins,
from the manifactury established in Paris by the renowned Gille
Gobelin. We had already in the 16th century a native manufactory
for this kind; under Frederik II it was first located in Elsinor, afterwards in Slangerup; Christian V removed it to Kjøge, where the
building still remains and from thence the general name of »Kjøge-
tapestry was derived. The manufacture was however discontinued

The south end—sitting.

under Christian **VI** being far too costly a branch of industry for the government of so small a land to support.

Whilst our eye still glides around the saloon it will be annected now by one, then another piece of the highly characteristic Rococo furniture found here: mirrors with magnificent carved and gilded frames of wood, tables rich in carving and gilding with slabs of marble, Florentine mosaics, or marquetry inlaid with rare woods, or covered with skilful Italian filigree work &c., which cannot fail to awaken our attention by the ability, which is frequently displayed in the execution of the work, even if the bizarre fancies of its masters should at times startle us. We will however particularly remark:

An ebony cabinet resting upon four twisted pillars and tastefully inlaid with flowers, birds, arabesques &c. in ivory and different sorts of wood. The interior of its doors are of plate-glass on which are painted trees; the interior recess of the cabinet is likewise ornamented with plate-glass, ivory &c. The date 1679 can be read in the inlaying. The frame of this piece of furniture is formed on the sides by two rows of secret drawers, and above and beneath by two broad drawers. This cabinet together with two gueridons, a mirror and a table of the same work as is found here are according to an old tradition Danish work.

In this cabinet, amongst other things, are found: a miniature bust in silver of Christian V standing upon a silver-gilt pedestal, the whole 10 inches high. — One in red wax, 5½ inches high. — An equestrian statuette painted in natural colours, ⅞ of an inch high, standing upon a marble column, 3½ inches high. Another equestrian statuette of gilded metal, 1 inch high, on a marble column, 4½ inches high (which like the former was executed by Jakob the son of the japanners).

A table. The slab is of olive-green Italian marble, down each side of which a strip of white marble is inlaid and in the centre a plate of white marble, upon which is engraved the crowned monogram of Christian V. The underpart (of gilded maple) consists of fantastic figures (telamons) as legs for the table. These as well as the frieze of the table are decorated with carvings. On the frieze is a rich garland of oak foliage and flowers; in the middle beneath the arms of Denmark and Hesse in a wreath of foliage and flowers.

For the rest we remark in this saloon:

A closet with dresses and state gala weapons. Among the dresses, of which many are richly embroidered in gold, the coronation-dress of Christian V (a Spanish cavalier's dress, white with gold) and the buff jerkin he wore in the battle of Lund must be distinguished. The iron sword, that hangs besides the last mentioned dress, was likewise the one borne by him in the Scanian war. — The gala weapons, namely three swords with enamelled diamond set hilts &c., are work of the most costly kind; notice particularly the hilt with the serpent and the heart —

A table.

the handle, ferrule and the spurs belonging to this set may be reckoned among the most excellent productions of the golden age of the art of enamel. We will lastly name from the contents of this closet a staff of command, the ball and terminal ferrule of which are of gold and decorated with diamonds.

Christian V was crowned in Frederiksborg church Juni 7th 1671. On this occasion the difference between the time past and the then esent was brought distinctly forward. With a view to this Frederik III had caused the coronation-chair, the closed royal crown and the rest of the regalia to be completed (of which more below), and the lex regia (the writ of absolutism in Denmark), drawn up by Peter Schumacher and subscribed by Frederik III November 14th 1665 and which had hitherto been kept secret, was then read aloud for the first time.

A cabinet with turned and carved objects in ivory, coral, amber &c., many of which are of considerable value as works of art. The most distinguished are:

A round ivory mug, whose spherical exterior is adorned with a well executed copy in relievo of one of Tenier's pictures. — Many groups of the utmost value (St. George slaying the dragon; the offering of Abraham; Romulus and Remus &c.) and other objects of coral. — Many caskets of amber (amongst which one 22 inches long, 13 inches broad and 14 inches high; upon the corners eight amber-figures, the sides and lid are ornamented with basrelievo in ivory and amber).

Upon two of the cabinets observe three japanned vases of wood. Amongst many different objects placed upon the tables remark: a drinkinghorn, formed from the horn of an ox, with cover and ornaments of silver. The escutcheon of Griffenfeld as count beautifully engraved upon a silver plate is placed upon its front. Count Griffenfeld presented the horn to Copenhagen his native place, and it was formerly preserved in the townhall for the use of the magistrates upon festive occasions.

A calendar of gilded metal made for Christian V by the celebrated Ole Romer (the discoverer of the velocity of light, born 1644, died 1710). — A mug of carved wood. With cover, handle and foot of embossed silver. The carving is done by Lars Berthelsen, who was parish-clerk at that time in the church of the Holy Ghost, Copenhagen.

Three large and magnificent articles of silver. Ornamented with gilding, engraved and embossed work. The principal part a globe (upon which are figures of Juno, Jupiter and Mars); can be separated so as to form a bowl, the interior of which is gilded, the exterior engraved; it is supported by a beautifully wrought figure. They have most probably been won as prizes for tilting.

A metal virginal (Spinet).

It consists of a green painted wooden case, that rests upon four legs, and contains two rows of metal keys; the upper row representing the semi-tones, and the lower the full-tones. Small mallets are used in playing it, and it has a range of three and a half octaves.

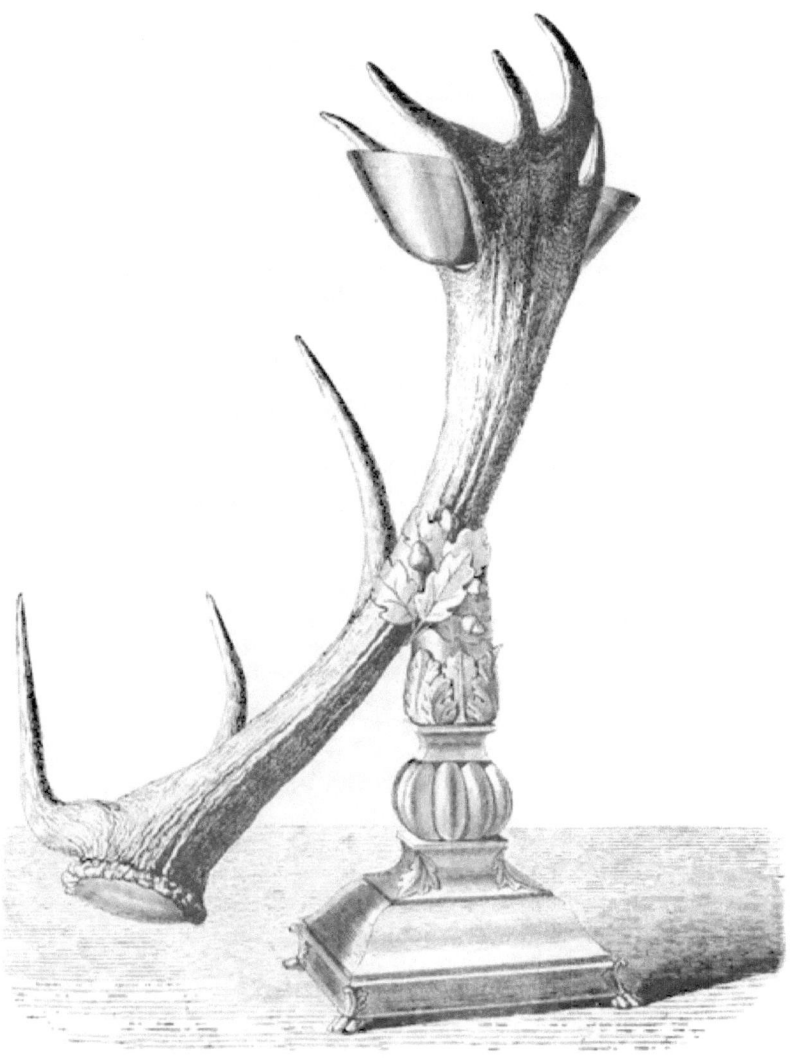

A hunting cup.

A hunting cup.

An oblong silvercup, gilded within, that rests on the tips of a deer's antlers (ten branches), from which it could be removed to the table when required for use.

Two hunting cups with covers, both formed of the antlers of deer. They are covered with gilded silver interiorly; a small spray of coral serves as knob upon the lid of one of them.

In the corner closet we notice a rich collection of hunting-weapons and other articles belonging to the chase: 22 fowling-pieces and pistols; 1 crossbow; 1 pole-axe; 2 hangers (the hilt and ferrule of the one beautifully carved from the horn of the rhino-ceros); 2 magnificent hunting knives in sheaths with silver gilt mountings and case; 1 small black hunting horn which was used in the German hunts; 2 falcon-hoods, the one set with real pearls and embroidered in gold; 1 hawking-bag &c.

If hawking has never played with us the rôle that it has in other places, nevertheless Denmark enjoyed no insignificent place in its history as the principal depot of the valuable Iceland falcon, that was first trained here and then sent as present from the Danish court to foreign princes. The last falcon was sent hence in 1806 to Portugal, and the last hawking-party in Denmark occurred March 1803 in honour of William duke of Gloucester, who was at that time the guest of the Danish court.

Christian V was a most passionate lover of field sports, which he pursued under many aspects: hunting with hounds, swanshooting, hawking &c. (a passion he inherited from his mo-ther), he was also an admirable marksman. In proof of this asser-tion the bone of an animal preserved in this closet can be adduced, which at a shooting feast in Randers, when crownprince, he twice shot through with his rifle at 30 ells distance, as it was held up between the fingers of one of the towns-men there present. An inscription upon the bone records the fact. — Another souvenir of his last hunt is found in this saloon over the door leading into the corridor, namely the antlers of a stag, which on the 19th of October 1698 in a hunt with hounds in the deer-park (»Dyrehaven« near Copenhagen) gored the king, who gave the »coup de grace«, so severely, that he never recovered the effects of it during the ten months he still lived.

In the glass-case: a number of miniatures, many enamelled, amongst which:

Christian V (6). — Charles XI of Sweden. — Michael Kory-buth Wysniowicki, king of Poland. — Louis XIV. — The elector

4

Friederich Wilhelm of Brandenburg. — Prince George and his consort, queen Anna of England. — Griffenfeld (by A. Prieur) &c. — 2 busts of Christian V in gold (borne as decorations, the one by Griffenfeld).

A falcon-hood.

The ribbon and the star of St. George, an excellent work, Christian V's decoration as knight of the garter.

In the front it shows St. George on horseback slaying the dragon; it is enamelled gold in open work, so that the reverse — grey Onyx upon which is carved St. George — shines through.

Four elephants (two of which are crystal) and one, a clear elephant upon a green ground (cameo).

The order of the elephant. The first trace of this order goes back to Christian I, who in the year 1457 founded a clerical brotherhood (a confraternity) the members of which wore as a sign of community a chain, which bore a medal with the Virgin on one side and an elephant on the other. We have no hint of the motive, which induced the adoption of the elephant as a symbol. Christian I as well as his immediate successors, Hans and Christian II, wore a chain with the elephant and are known to have conferred it on others as a particular badge. After the reformation the

The obverse.   The reverse.

Christian V's star of St. George.

order remained for some time in abeyance (on account of its catholic origin) but was again revived by Frederik II with an elephant alone as the badge of the order. Christian IV joined to it the armed hand until 1634. From this time it has been borne alone, in white enamel with blue housing and decorated with the kings monogram and diamonds, under Christian IV in a gold chain, under Frederik III (who September 23rd 1663 commanded all the knights of the order to place a tower upon the back of the elephant) in a blue ribbon round the neck. The present form dates from Christian V, who December 1st 1693 consolidated its rules. The badge of the order is now a white enamelled elephant in gold with a tower of red enamel upon its

4*

back, and ornamented with a diamond cross on the side. It is borne on the right hip in a broad blue silk ribbon, which hangs over the left shoulder. On the right side of the breast an eight-rayed star, with the cross in its centre, is worn. The dress of the order is a white Spanish cavalier's dress, a mantle of crimson velvet lined with white satin, and cap with white and red plumes.

A knife; with haft and sheath of gold excellently enamelled. Many smaller objects of excellent workmanship in silver, gold,

The order of the elephant.

crystal and precious stones (a small note-book with calender in a gold-filigree binding; sewing-implements in a crystal-case &c).

A seal for wax-impressions of the escutcheon of the Danish kingdom engraved on two silverplates set in bronze, on the one, the obverse: the king on the throne, surrounded by the three lions; on the other, the reverse: the arms of the kingdom, as used in the earliest stage of absolutism. The escutcheon of Denmark in enamel (by Barbette, 1694).

In addition we will name as characteristic illustration of the times: a piece of smelted gold which the landgrave of Hesse-Homburg himself made from a piece of lead. A portion of the original lead, from which the gold was transmuted lies beside it. Presented to Christian V 1695. — Finally we will point out:

A little picture of Christian IV in a frame of gilded wood. Behind we read the following verse:

> Min Sönne-Sön og storste Naffne,
> Du ligner mig i Mact og Moed:
> Ach lad ded nu min leffning gaffne,
> Du oc som jeg est Naade-Goed!
> 1685.

(My grandson and greatest name-sake, thou art my equal in power and spirit, oh! let it now profit my daughter, that thou, as I, art merciful and good.)

This picture was sent from her prison to Christian V by Eleonora Kristina Ulfeld, when she had learned, that her envious enemy Sophia Amalia was dead in February 1685. She relates in the wonderful history of her sufferings (Jammersmindet which she wrote in prison), that she had herself painted the picture and gilded the frame. The verse, which she had likewise composed and written, was her petition for liberty, which was finally granted her in May 1685, after she had undergone a severe and strict confinement from August 1663. The rest of her life — 13 years — was passed in Maribo cloister. She died March 16th 1698 aged almost 77 years. A beautiful souvenir of the aged lady's gratitude, as well as of her persevering industry the collection possesses in:

the portrait of Christian V, which she embroidered during her residence in Maribo. It is embroidered with silk. The frame on the contrary, which shows the four emblems of royalty: the crown, the sword, the sceptre and the globe, in raised work, is wrought with gold thread. It is with the frame 56 inches high and 44 inches broad. Upon that part of the picture, nearest the edge of the enclosing frame, she has worked the following verse:

> See her en Konge goed, en englesielet Mand,
> Der i Gudsfrögt med Ret regierer Folck oe Land,
> See her en stoer Monarck, hvis Hofved wærdig war,
> At hand i tusind Aar Allwerdens Croner bar.

(See here a good king, a man with an angels mind, who in piety justly governs the people and land; see here a great monarch, whose head were worthy that he for a thousand years wore all the crowns of the world.)

Of the other pictures on the wall we will here notice:

Many portraits of Christian V and queen Charlotta Amalia. — Prince George in the dress of the order of the garter (marble relievo). — A painting in waters colours representing Copenhagen in the time of Christian V. — Christian V as a child (the originals of the cannons therein delineated stands under the picture on the floor). — Sophia Amalia Moth. — An unfinished painting, in which are Christian V, Ulrich Frederik Gyldenlove and the earl of Oldenburg. — Many pictures in relievo in ivory (medallionportraits, landscapes &c.). — And further Christian V in profile carved in box wood &c. —

Before leaving this saloon we will rest a moment by the little anchor, that hangs by the fire place. It shows traces of having been covered with gilding and underneath we read a little verse of Kingo, in which it is said:

To sterkke Anker brast og maatte bölger vige,
Men ieg holt fast oppaa Monarkens tvilling Rige.

Two strong anchors broke and had to drive before the waves,
But I held fast to the monarchs twin-kingdom.

Tradition states that this anchor saved the kings ship during a storm by Christianso near Bornholm (1687); a medal was struck to perpetuate the memory of this event and is preserved in the collection of coins and medals.

The tower room

is hung with figured Chinese plush upon a gold ground. The ceiling is of wood divided into panels, with attached pendants; it is also decorated with painting and gilding.

In the glass cabinet: a large goblet and two large oval tureens with covers of gold enamelled and thickly set with cameos and precious stones, that belong partly to the ancient and partly to the more modern time.

(We will here only incidentally quote a tradition, of defective authenticity, which asserts, that one of the tureens formed part of the baptismal present given by the States General to Ulfeld during his embassy to Holland 1647, when the whole of the States General stood godfathers to the son Leonora Kristina bore during their residence at L'Hague and who after the wish of the numerous godfathers received in baptism the name Leo Belgicus).

A gold jug ornamented with embossed work and enamel. — An enamelled gold beaker. — Two bowls of Jade ornamented with enamel &c.

These bowls are by reason of their size exceedingly valuable since jade, which is greatly monopolized by the Chinese (who call

The Wismar goblet.

it »Yu.) and only used for rare and magnificent objects, has always stood at a very high price.

A very rare collection (12 items) of cut crystal articles of different sizes. We will confine ourselves to particularizing the so-called Wismar goblet.

The main piece, which bears the form of a flying fish, is by help of enamelled, ruby-decorated goldrings composed in part of somewhat large crystals: it is nearly 13 inches long, and borne by two delphins inter-twined, whose heads rest upon a dish (like all the rest of crystal) about 11 inches long. On the taking of Wismar December 13th 1675 it was presented by the Swedish general as a sign of submission to the conqueror Christian V; hence its name.

Further costly objects (9 pieces) of lithoxylon (petrefied wood) onyx, serpentine, jasper, heliotrope and agate with enamelled goldsettings &c.

Many cut glassarticles, amongst which a champagneglass 20 inches high with the following verse engraved upon it:

> Wer mit Bachus kompt ins Spiel,
> Seh sich für und trau nicht viel,
> Nimpt er dir dein Kopff nur ein,
> So seind die Füsze nimmer dein.

Upon the walls hangs: A bust portrait of the brother in law of Christian V, Charles landgrave of Hesse. It is 12 inches high and 11 inches broad, oval and composed of stones. The portrait, which, in relievo, is formed of crystal, agate, lapis lazuli, onyx, cornelian and chalcedony, rises from a ground of agate. The frame is gilded metal.

Notice also here: A round can of white and blue Chinese porcelain with mountings of silver and a silver crown in the middle of the cover, that rests upon intricate wreathings of the name of queen Charlotta Amalia. It belonged to her and was brought as a present in the first ship, that sailed from Denmark to China.

It was under Christian V that commerce in Denmark sprung properly to life, and that the Danes began to employ their own shipping in the merchant service. Before this all important trade had been left at first to the Hanse and afterwards to the Dutch and English; and the attempt that was made by Christian IV to call to life an independent Danish commerce (by the appointment of guard-ships, the institution of an East-India Co. &c.) did not materially prosper, in part owing to his last unfortunate war. During the miseries that Denmark endured under Frederik III it sunk lower and lower; but now, when years had passed in peace, and Christian V by an ordinance of May 24th 1671, in which he revived the idea of the guard-ships of Christian IV, had encouraged Danish merchants to build vessels adapted for long voyages, granting them trade **privileges and exemptions from** custom dues in proportion to **the size of the ship**; when St. Thomas and St. Jan (1672) were **acquired** &c. -- then by degrees Danish trade ex- , panded mightily; **so much the more**, as the greater part of the other commercial **states of Europe** at the end of the 17th century were entangled **in a war that clogged all their trade and commerce.**

Lastly let us call attention to the pictures hung in the tower room:

Many portraits of Christian V. — A good portrait of Griffen- feld. — Two paintings, the one of which shows us the coronation **of Christian V in the chapel of the palace of Frederiksborg**, the other represents him as presiding over the supreme **court. — A double portrait (on a fluted ground)** of Frederik IV **as prince and his sister Sophia Hedevig. —** The electress Vilhelmine Ernestine. **— A representation of the Danish crowns.** — **A number of small paintings (portraits, flowerpieces** &c.) mounted in frames of silver **filigree and executed by** the princess Sophia Hedevig. — **Further a number of relievo portraits in ivory.**

Amongst the furniture preserved here (4 tables, a cabinet japanned and **inlaid with mosaic, many carved chairs** &c.) we will specify **a** table, **whose slab is covered with embroidery**, the work of queen Charlotta **Amalia, bearing allusion to a little** mystification she **was once** the **subject of at the card table.**

After we **have thus made acquaintance with the** ground floor and the most **important objects contained there**, we will continue our wandering **up the winding-staircase to the first** floor. Upon **the way a series of historical portraits glide** past us:

Simon Paulli, physician and botanist, who died 1680, and his **wife Elizabeth Fabritius.** The learned Villum Vorm, who died **1704. — Kort** Adeler, admiral. Griffenfeld (3 times). — **The mother of Griffenfeld,** Marie **Schumacher,** born Motzfeld. — Niels **Juel, admiral.** — **His** brother, **Jens Juel.** — Thomas Bartholin, a celebrated **physician,** who **died 1680. — Ole Borch, a** renowned chemist, who **died** 1690. **— Tormod Torfæus, a learned** historian, born **in** Iceland **1636,** died **in Copenhagen 1719. —** Erik Pontoppidan, **a** clergyman celebrated **for his learning, died** 1678. — Henrik Ernst, **a** learned lawyer, died 1665. **— P. Reetz, a** statesman, died 1674. — Lambert v. Haven, renowned **architect, died** 1695. — Adam Olearius, placed with duke Frederik III of Holstein-Gottorp. Henrik Gerner, bishop, who died **1700. —** Marie Schumacher (Griffenfeld's sister) **and** her husband burgomaster **Fogh** Frederik Alefeldt, count of Langeland, statesman. — Oluf Rosenkrants, a learned lawyer, who died 1685, and many others.

The Rose.

Such was the name of a large oblong space in the centre of the second floor, which perhaps in days long fled had its decorations of one kind or another, but which in that case, had gradually fallen a sorrowful victim to the tooth of time; for before the new arrangement of the museum it consisted merely of four walls (sparely hung with paintings) within which for a long period the state-lottery held its yearly drawings. The space is now somewhat less than formerly, but as a compensation it has received a fitting-up and arrangement, which give it a suitable place in the historical series, so that it forms a transition from the time of Christian V to that of Frederik IV. In its furniture, portraits and the rest of its decorations it represents both of these monarchs; we will therefore name at once the articles it conserves:

Upon the three walls four tapestries of unequalled beauty and rarity.

These hangings were first brought from the lumber room and hang up here in the present day. Three of them consist of a lilac silk texture upon which mythological representations after the pictures of Raphael and other renowned painters (arabesques, flowers, different animals &c.) are embroidered with gold and silver thread, and painted with colours. The 4th (to the right) is of gold moire with silk embroidered medallions, that represent scenes from the history of Greece &c. These tapestries date beyond doubt from the second journey of Frederik IV to Italy.

Under the ceiling, that is now decorated with four paintings of Krock (1, Juno and Fortuna; 2, Fortuna) and of Coiffre (3, Venus, who dresses, while Cupid sits in her chariot; 4, Secresy), there hangs a chandelier of rock-crystal and cut iron, of extraordinary value. After the tradition a gift to Christian V from Louis XIV the time that he supporting the police of Griffenfeld tried to prevent the Scanian war.

In the middle of the floor (at present an inlaid floor of oakwood) is a table with an arm-chair belonging to it.

Until our own days these objects were used by the king when he opened the supreme court of justice and presided amongst the judges. With the exception of the slab of the table, the seat and back of the chair, which are ornamented with red velvet and gold embroidery (now somewhat worn and faded) both pieces are

The Rose

plated with silver. On the back of the chair rest is seen the Norwegian lion with the curved axe. — From a mark engraved in the silver covering we discover that these objects date from October 1715 (the birthday of Frederik IV) and it is said they were a present to the king from his last queen, Anna Sophia. This is indicated amongst other things by the placing of the Norwegian arms upon the chair: the silver was brought from the shaft belonging to Anna Sophia in the Kongsberg silvermines.

Of the rest of the furniture that is specially noticeable:

A large well-preserved c a b i n e t with a rich inlaying of mosaic. — Two m i r r o r s with gilded frames, of which one is most beautifully carved with figures and rich mountings. — Carved c h a i r s with figured gilt leather covers.

Upon the walls:

Portraits of Christian V and queen Charlotta Amalia, set in larges, somewhat heavy, yet richly carved frames of gilded wood. — The landgrave Charles of Hesse. — Prince George (many times). — The princess Sophia Hedevig. — Queen Ulrikke Eleonora (Christian V's sister and mother of Charles XII of Sweden). — Frederik IV (painted by Rigaud, the famous court painter of Louis XIV) and others. Further: A marble statuette of Christian V in his coronation mantle, 22 inches high. — An ivory equestrian statuette of Christian V. Two marble busts of Frederik IV and his first queen, Louise.

Christian V died August 25th 1699.

The time of Frederik IV (1699—1730).

During many years an ill feeling had grown up between the kings of Denmark and the dukes of Gottorp, whose personal interest constantly set more and more in a direction inimical to Denmark, showing itself, amongst other aspects, in their pertinacious endeavours to germanise Sleswick. Frederik III had sought to improve their relationship by a marriage between his daughter Frederikke Amalia and duke Christian Albrecht; which union however brought no change for the better; and when in 1675 Christian V forced from his brother in law the agreement of Rendsburg, which was more in harmony with a wise and calculating policy than with the requirements of justice, the gulf between them could no longer be bridged over. It is true that during the latter years of Christian V the relations between him and Christian Albrecht were apparently more tolerable, but when in 1694 Christian

BO-

Frederik IV.

Albrecht died and was succeeded by his son, duke Frederik IV, the tension increased daily; the young duke married Hedvig Sophia, the sister of Charles XII of Sweden, entered into alliance with Sweden, raised fortresses &c., and after the death of Christian V it had extended so far that the sword only could cut the knot. The alliance of Denmark with Peter the great and Augustus of Saxony was not however sufficient against the help that Gottorp received from other powers, particularly from Sweden, and in the peace of Travendal (August 1700) king Frederik was obliged to acknowledge the sovereignity of the duke and to pay him a large sum of money as well. The mutual illwill continued to smoulder and during the eleven years war (1709—1720) with Sweden it burst into a flame, when the ducal government after the battle of Gadebusch had opened the fortress of Tønning to the Swedish general Magnus Stenbock. The consequence was that king Frederik IV took again Gottorp's portion of the dukedom of Sleswick, which in the peace of Frederiksborg 1720 was acknowledged by Sweden and guarantied by France and England for ever .

This was the great achievement of king Frederik IV's policy; but in many other respects he was worthy of being held in honorable remembrace by posterity; he was laborious and a good householder; had a tender heart for the oppressed peasantry, a warm interest in the enlightenment of the people, in commerce and industry, and had also a lively taste for art. During his stay in Italy — the last time 1708—9 — his eyes were ever open to art-objects, and Rosenborg possesses many memorials of this.

Frederik IV was twice married, 1, with Louise (princesse of Mecklenburg Güstrow), who died 1721, 2, with Anna Sophia (daughter of the Grandchancellor Count Konrad Reventlow), who died 1743.

We make acquaintance with the period of Frederik IV on this floor, in the Rose (see before), the mirror room, the north end-saloon and the north-east tower-room; and in the uppermost story in the knights hall and the glass-room.

The mirror room

lies in the west tower by the side of the Rose with which it is connected by a short passage. Its walls, ceiling and an oblong circle in the middle of the floor are covered with plate-glass. The rest of the floor has a beautifully designed inlaying of wood and bone of different colours.

is connected with the »Rose« by a passage, hung with gold-figured leather, in which we find a number of portraits: Frederik IV (twice). — Queen Louise. — Charles XII. — The same with his sister Hedevig Sophia (as children upon one canvas, painted by Ehrenstrahl). — The sister of the same, Hedevig Sophia. — The sister of the same, Ulrikka Eleonora the younger. — The admiral Tordenskjold. — General Poul Løvenørn. — The painter Heinrich Krock. — Henrik Meyercrone (a statesman, who died 1707) painted by Rigaud. — The renowned courtier Frederik Walther. — A bust in gilded metal of the czar Peter the great. — We notice further in this passage: an ironstove (from 1729) the upper part of which as well as the foot is of Delft-ware; also a very beautiful cabinet with inlaying of Florentine mosaic.

The saloon itself was formerly called the »Brown Apartment« perhaps because the wainscoting of the black, gold filleted panels is brown. The walls are for the rest covered with hautelisse tapestry representing scenes from mythology. The ceiling is wainscoted and painted. The heat-reflecting balls by the fire place, before which there is an embroidered screen, are of silver. Above the chimney-piece hangs a painting representing general Magnus Stenbock, who sits surrounded by poultry with a paper in his hand on which is written: »Herr lasz deinen gefangenen Los« (Lord set they prisoner free). It was painted for Frederik IV by Stenbock during his imprisonment (1713) as a sort of petition for freedom.

After Stenbock, who as before mentioned had escaped to Tønning May 16th 1713, had been obliged to surrender with his whole army, he was brought to Copenhagen, where at first he was allowed to dwell in his own house and very mildly treated. Not before it was discovered that he misused this freedom by entering into a correspondence with the enemies of Denmark, was he placed under stricter surveillance in the citadel of Copenhagen, where he died February 23rd 1717.

Upon the walls we find also the following pictures:

Many portraits of Frederik IV of different sizes (2 in oil, 4 in water-colour on paper, 1 relievo in wax). — Queen Louise (3). — Queen Anna Sophia. — Princess Sophia Hedevig. — 3 small portraits of the brothers of Frederik IV: Christian (who died 1695), William and Charles. — The anointment of Frederik IV and queen Louise in the chapel of Frederiksborg (painted by the younger Grotschilling, who died as surveyor of the artchamber

1737). — The Lying in State (castrum doloris) of Frederik IV in the castle chapel of Odense (water-colour by Schnitter).

The furniture of the time of Frederik IV evinces in the highest degree his artistic tastes and gives an excellent exposition of the rococo style, above all as it has developed itself in Italy in the beginning of the 18th century; for this king brought from thence much of the furniture now preserved in his rooms in Rosenborg. In this saloon we will specially notice:

A large, and in spite of time's distructive finger, still beautiful ebony cabinet. The under part is formed of boldly carved figures in gilded wood; and it is further ornamented with metal figures, inlaying of different coloured stones and with small scriptural representations in water-colour (under glass) upon the drawers. — (On the top of this cabinet are now placed two particularly rare Persian wine-jugs of porcelain with fine drawings in gold (flowers &c. upon a blue ground); around the slender neck of each two handles of silver-gilt; upon the covers the crowned monogram of queen Louise in silvergilt.)

Many smaller cabinets inlaid with mosaic &c. — Three time-pieces (temple-formed) ornamented with tortoise-shell, embossed silver ornaments, enamel — even with pearls and precious stones, executed in Florence by order of Frederik IV.

A medicine-chest of tortoise-shell ornamented with plates and figures of embossed silver; above upon a pyramide mounted in silver a little watch.

An extraordinary beautiful table with slab of exceedingly fine Florentine mosaic (fruits, flowers, flying birds &c.). The legs of the table are twined and richly ornamented with gilded metal work.

A table, a pair of gueridones and a mirror, whose frame, as well as the before mentioned objects, is of box-wood inlaid with various other woods in the Japanese style.

A table of fine inlaid work, upon which stands a tea-urn of blue and white porcelain with a set of six cups, that are lined with silver. On the cover of the urn is the monogram of Frederik IV; tradition says they were brought home by the first ship, that sailed to and from China, as a present to the king.

Under the ceiling hangs a very costly chandelier of cut rock-crystal.

In the closet to the right: dresses, weapons &c.

Of the four dresses preserved here we would draw particular attention to that of crimson velvet with the rich silver-embroidery.

Upon the sides under the arms the skirt is laid in six folds (in
the midst of the folds on the left side a slit is cut, through which
to pass the sword. The waistcoat is of blue silvered material.
It was worn by Frederik IV as a bridegroom December 5th 1695.

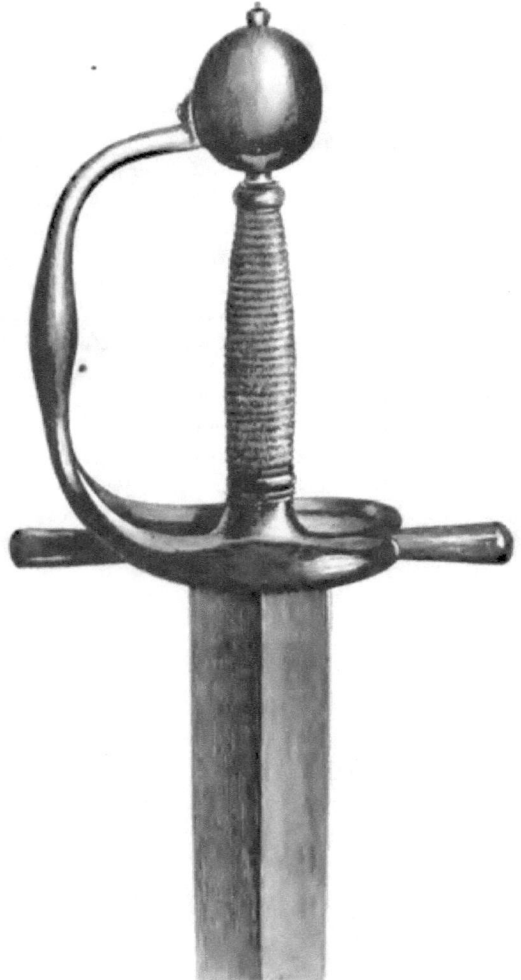

The sword of Charles XII.

The most striking weapons are: The sword of Charles XII.
It is a sword simply mounted, about 42 inches long, with brass

5

hilt and black leather sheath. Given by king Charles to the valiant colonel Kruse, who with 200 dragons on the 9th of March 1716 threw himself upon the Swedish avant guard of 600 horsemen, led by king Charles himself, and strove long and bravely before, succumbing to superiority of numbers, he finally submitted. — Further: A broad sword with gold hilt. Frederik IV's double monogram upon the basket-hilt. — Two hangers, also with gold hilts, which are decorated with pearls, rubies and the Norwegian lion in enamel. They belonged to prince Charles, the brother of Frederik IV. - A hunting-knife with an agate handle, on which is a setting of garnets. — A sword with a gold hilt and an agate clasp, both parts somewhat bent and injured.

This happened by a fall the king had, when in 1729 he was present at the casting of some cannons in the ·Cannon-foundry« (Gjethuset); on which occasion a mould unluckily burst and the fluid mass of metal streamed out and set fire to the raised platform, upon which the king sat. As in the perplexity he hastened down the steep and narrow backstairs, he tripped and was precipitated from so considerable a height, that he could scarcely have escaped with life, had not his valet caught him in his outstretched arms. Nevertheless how severe the fall must have been, can be seen from the injury sustained by the sword here spoken of, and which was worn by the king at the time; it is also known that he never recovered from its effects.

A brace of pistols; the stocks of ivory and ornamented with silver-gilt mountings; the tubes bronzed and inlaid with gold. A present from Louis XIV to Frederik IV. Beside these we find in the closet a great many other fire-arms (pistols & guns) of which some, the work of the renowned gunsmiths Frederik Ostermann and Henrik Kappel, are exquisitely finished.

Among the numerous walking-sticks (19) in this closet we will notice two: a tortoiseshell stick with a gold knob, upon which we read in enamel: mes mouvemens sont caché , and a cane with a diamond mounted enamelled gold knob. A present to Frederik IV from his sister Sophia Hedevig, who herself enamelled the knob.

We further find in this closet a magnificent copy of the ·lex regia· bound in gold embroidered red velvet, that was presented to Frederik IV, when printed for the first time:

In the closet in the south wall we notice:

The Sleswick merorial goblets i. e. The Eiderstream-goblet and the Allegiance-goblet; they are both of gold and weigh with the covers, the first 47 ounces, the last 38.

1, The Eiderstream-goblet. Upon the lid is a winged genius blowing a trumpet with the inscription:

Gud, som gav vor Konge Fred,
Lad dem Begge blive ved.

The Eiderstream-goblet.

(God, who gave peace to our king, preserve them both.) The inscription upon the front medallion (from 1720) points the Eider as the boundary river of Denmark:

Fra Kong Friderichs Arve Rige
Eyder-Strömmen ej vil vige;

5*

(From king Fridrich's hereditary monarchy the Eiderstream will not recede.) The medal behind shows the fortress of Cronbourg and bears the inscription:

.   Dend Told Som Bör Told 1720.

(Customs to him to whom customs are due.) Between these two medallions, in engraved and embossed work, is on one side a representation of the marriage of Frederik IV and Anna Sophia, and of her coronation upon the other; also the following inscription on the first:

> Af Guds og Kongens haand
> Blev Knyttet dette baand.

(By the hand of God and of the king this tie was bound), and this upon the second:

> Gud Sette evig fast
> Kong Fridrichs Arve Throne,
> Som Skenkte sin Gemahl
> Sit Hjerte, Spir og Crone.

(May God preserve for ever king Fridrich's hereditary throne, who bestowed on his spouse his heart, sceptre and crown.)

2, The Allegiance-goblet. On the front it bears a representation of the ceremony of taking the oaths of allegiance in Gottorp castle with the inscriptions written on a white enamelled grund, above:

> Stænderne i Fyrstend: Schlesvig hylde Kong Friderich IV
> 1721 d. 4 Sept.

(The inhabitants of the principality of Slesvick pay homage to king Friederich IV 1721 the 4th of Sept.) underneath:

> At anden halve part
> Af Schlesvig Danmarks bleev,
> Den fierde Friderich
> Med fliid igjennem dreev.

(That the other half of Sleswick became a part of Denmark Friederich IV with energy effectuated.) Behind appears the portrait of the king with the date October 11th 1721 (his birth day) upon a white enamelled ground, as also the inscription:

> Det halve er forbi,
> Gud fylde hundred aar!
> En bedre Souverain
> Vor Norden aldrig faar.

(The half is passed, may God fill a hundred years! A better king our North never will gain.) On the sides between are two medallions commemorative of the fall of Charles XII with these inscriptions:

The Allegiance-goblet.

Den Svenske Love falt
For Norske Lovens Fod;
Der midste hand Sit Lif
Og Sidste helte Blod.

(The Swedish lion fell at the foot of Norway's lion; there he lost his life and last heroic blood) and

Saa var hans Skæbne;
Friderichshall d. 11 December 1718.

(Such was his fate; Friderichshald the 11th December 1718.)

It was formerly the custom over the whole of Europe, as is well known, to attach the memory of remarkable events with such goblets; in Windsoor castle, e. g., a Union-goblet is preserved to commemorate the union of England and Scotland. The goblets here described connect themselves with the peace of Frederiksborg, by which amongst other advantages Denmark recovered the privilege, which she had lost by the peace of Brømsebro (1645), of demanding toll of Swedish ships, that passed the Sound, and got the incorporation of the old Danish country of Sleswick acknowledged and guaranteed.

Between these two goblets stands a large gold goblet with an enamelled and diamond decorated regal crown upon the cover and the monogram of Frederik IV in diamonds upon the side. It rests upon three lions, each of which bears a blank shield, at present without name or escutcheon. It weighs about 137 oz.

Count U. A. Holstein, married to a half-sister of Anna Sophia Reventlov, had helped the king to carry off this lady from Klauslolm Juni 26th 1712, and when she was crowned queen of Denmark, he received this goblet from his illustrious brother in law as a souvenir of this. After the loss of our fleet in 1807 it was given as a subscription towards a new fleet to the finances and would also have been melted into money, but Frederik VI redeemed it and thus preserved it to posterity. —

Eight gold goblets, partly ornamented with the monogram of Frederik IV, partly engraved ornaments and are finished in an exceedingly beautiful manner: notice particularly two shallow goblets (mustache's goblets), that are distinguishable from the extraordinary taste and delicacy of their ornamentation.

A multitude of objects, of value as excellent specimens of the art of that day in various directions:

A toilet set (looking-glass, a pair of candle sticks, a brush and seven boxes) of silver with unusually rich and tasteful enamel. It belonged to Sophia Hedevig. — A travelling-case of gold with spoon, knife and fork and four small spaces; bears the monogram of Frederik IV in enamel. — Two large cut ruby glasses with covers, presented to Frederik IV by Ernst duke of Saxe-Lauenburg 1714. — A large bowl of Icelandic obsidian (volcanic glass). A silver sheep stands in the middle of the hid;

it is decorated with the painted miniature portraits of Frederik IV
and Anna Sophia, surrounded by rubies and garnets. — Two

A large gold goblet.

cans of cut crystal with enamelled covers. — A toilet
»medicin-chest«, containing 7 small cut bottles, the largest in

the centre, all ornamented with diamonds and finely finished silver garlands twisted round them. — A little enamelled jewel-case, richly set with diamonds &c. — An ivory fan, ornamented with exceedingly fine painting; Frederik IV brought it home with him from Italy as a present to his queen Louise. — Many articles of amber, amongst others two small flacons with mountings and chains of gold. — A bowl, formed of an enormous garnet (in the lid, which is formed of numerous small garnets, are read the crowned initials S. H.) with two handles formed of green enamelled serpents; it belonged to Sophia Hedevig. — Two large pearls, the one in the form of a swan with diamond wings, the other in that of a lamb. — A silver tree with green enamelled leaves and six emeralds of considerable size, cut in the form of clusters of grapes. — Two Moors of ebony with bows and arrows of gold, decorated with precious stones. — The portrait of Frederik IV, set in a pin with frame and crown of diamonds, and many small portraits with similar settings. — A lady's mirror in a broad enamelled frame, richly inlaid with Bohemian and other stones; according to tradition a present from Anna, queen of England. — One smaller, enamelled and ornamented with rose-diamonds. — Two pyramidal inkstands in gold, the larger belonged tho Frederik IV, the smaller to his sister Sophia Hedevig.

A pack of cards; the different colours and the count-cards are executed in silk embroidery upon paper; it belonged to queen Anna Sophia.

Two purses embroidered in gold and silver thread by the princess Sophia Hedevig. — Seven of the small paintings of this princess (landscapes, portraits, flower-pieces); five of these are in finely finished frames of silver filigree, the other two in silvergilt frames with enamelled gold decorations, diamonds and rubies.

The little oval mirror, placed in the centre of one of these paintings, tells us an anecdote: When Frederik IV after the oath of fealty in Gottorp visited his sister in Vemmetofte, where she resided, she presented him with this picture as a birthday present (see the date upon the picture) adding at the same time, that he could no longer complain of the unlucky painter's want of skill in hitting off a portrait — for he could himself see what an excellent likeness it was!

A small China cup and saucer, decorated with reference to the peace of Frederiksborg. They belonged to a large collection, which Frederik IV caused to be made in China as a sort oi memorial set.

Lastly a quantity of glassarticles (goblets, beakers, decanters), whose cut escutcheons and inscriptions have reference to the history of that time. Of these we will name a large beaker with a cover, in which are trophies and the following carving:

On the one side, the monogram of Charles XII, upon the other Hercules with the club between two pillars. Above — this inscription: Non hæc vltima meta laborum; underneath — this: XII labores Herevlei. Around in twelve oval rings: Desc. in Seel 1700. — Narva 1700. — Traidune 1701. — Pax Traventh. — Riga 1701. · Clissow 1702. — Tohrun 1703. — Lemberg 1704. — Grodno 1705. — Fravstad 1706. — Pax Altranst 1706. — Pultows.

We will now leave the saloon and open the carved oak doors immediately to the left, that lead in to the

tower room.

· This room still shows traces of an earlier decoration more magnificent than tasteful, namely Chinese relief-figures of lacquered work on the ceiling and walls, and among them costly stones, turquoise &c. — The eye will however quickly wander in search of some other object, but will find difficulty in deciding where to rest, for everywhere it falls upon numerous flowers of art, each of which deserves particular attention.

We notice here a costly set of furniture, chairs, mirrors, tables and cabinets, all covered with beautiful embossed silver-plates. — A chandelier of rock-crystal for eight lights.

Of portraits we remark: Frederik IV (by Denner); .queen Louise (by Wahl); Magnus Berg (a renowned sculptur, born in Norway 1666, died 1739).

We find upon the walls a number of objects, the work of the last named artist (37), works in ivory. Biblical and allegorical representations, many of which are excellent both as regards the composition and the design (notice for ex: the Scourging of Christ &c.). Besides these we find upon the walls a number of relief-works in ivory (portraits &c.).

Upon the silver-cabinet is placed: 1, a drinkinghorn, formed of an elephants tooth (22 inches long); 2, one of the horn of a rhinoceros (20 inches long). The last mentioned, which is lined with silver-gilt, has upon the middle two silver-gilt rings that, in an oblique position, hold it to the silver-gilt foot, which is 7½ inches high, in the form of a warrior, with bow and arrows, kneeling with the drinkinghorn upon his neck.

In the cabinet to the left: many objects carved and turned in ivory.

Amongst these two works executed by Magnus Stenbock in prison (1714), namely a box and a goblet, round which a serpent is entwined. Likewise two specimens of turners-work by the czar Peter the Great: a box with his bust upon the cover, in relievo, crowned with a laurel wreath, and a large covered goblet, upon which are many heads and arabesques, turned in relievo. Both these were given to Frederik IV by the czar during his residence in Denmark (from July to October 1716).

Many exceedingly tasteful articles in Genoese filigree- and coral-work &c. resulting from the journey of Frederik IV in Italy. — Silvercups, nautilus &c. — A large toilet-set of silver (18 articles), that belonged to the sister of Charles XII, Hedevig Sophia (who was married to duke Frederik IV of Gottorp, of whom we have before spoken, and who fell in Poland on the battle-field of Klissow 1702).

Notice further, placed on the outside of the said cabinet: A staff of a »runner« of ivory, 49 inches long, composed of ten ivory tubes, that move upon an iron pin. After tradition turned by Magnus Stenbock and used by his »runner« for the furtherance of a secret correspondance, which was however discovered and made the ground of his stricter imprisonment.

In the cabinet to the right: A silver equestrian statuette of Frederik IV, on a pedestal likewise of silver. The whole 14½ inches high. On the pedestal the arms of the provinces in enamel, surrounded by the motto of the king: Deus Mihi Adjutor. It was presented to the king by queen Louise as a new years gift 1701 and was the work of the royal goldsmith Andreas Normann.

An allegorical representation of Frederik IV as the Conqueror, in silver.

It bears allusion to the peace of Frederiksborg and is executed by Peter Klein. The king, in the act of being crowned by the goddess of victory, treads »Mischief« under his feet. Below, the lion with the drawn sword and the arms of the northern kingdoms. Among the many inscriptions upon the pedestal notice particularly that under the bas-relief Sleswick, who, kneeling, reaches out the Sleswick shield to Denmark, by whom the arms of the whole kingdom are held:

Huad Fiendens List fra Danmark reev,
Kong Friderich tilbage dreev.
1720.

What guile of fob from Denmark tore,
King Frederick did again restore.
1720.

A large silver goblet with a cover, 16 inches high;
on this the Norwegian lion with the crooked halberd. Outside
the cover as well as on the goblet itself is a series of Danish-
Norwegian and Swedish coins, from the time of Frederik IV and
Charles XII, and an engraved explanation of the more or less
happy condition of the northern kingdoms at that time, borne out
by reference to the coinage, good or bad, minted in each land.

A silver cup used by Peter the Great during his sojourn in
Copenhagen (1716). — A series of historical silver cups,
amongst which one made in 1713 of Russian copecks as a souvenir of Stenbocks defeat, as it is said in the inscription on the cup:

Naer Gadebuscher Schlacht, als Steenbock Tönning nam,
De Zaar Mit Sinem Swarm toerst in Holsteen Kam,
De Mit Der Sachsen Heer dat Gantze Land Dorch Streken,
Word ik To Preetz Gemaakt ut Russischen Copeken
Tom Denkmahl &c.

Upon the cabinets: Many japanned vases of wood. —
A silver horse. —

The knight's-hall and glass-room see below.

Frederik IV died October 12th 1730.

From the time of Christian VI (1730—1746).

The government of king Christian VI has impressed itself on
the memory of the Danish people with a peculiar sensation of
coldness and discomfort. A sovereign pair, who by an impassable
barrier of stiff and heartless etiquette had distanced themselves far
from the mass of the people; a court, whose extravagance and
glitter presented a strange contrast to the puritanical humility and
sanctity of mind and manners, they required not only of those,
who approached their person, but without exception of all; Ger-
manism obtruding, spreading and mixing in every concern; the
wretchedness of the peasantry — by such gradations of misery is
this period usually depicted, so that it is scarcely possible to perceive, that nevertheless it has its bright side also; that intrest was
shown for trade and industry and manufactures, for science and

Christian VI.

art in many directions, for the enlightenment of the public, for the advancement of the fleet (count Frederik Danneskjold-Samsø) &c.

Christian VI was by nature an honest, benevolent, right thinking man, and his haughty German queen Sophia Magdalena (princess of Brandenburg Kulmbach, who died 1770), has notwithstanding her claims also to a fair place in the memory of posterity as the benefactress of the Danish peasantry, since she made the first step towards freeing them from their bondage by exempting from villeinage those on her estate of Hirschholm, September 16th 1761.

The articles of the time of Christian VI are found in two rooms, a larger and a smaller one, on the otherside of the passage. The entrance is by a door opposite the tower-room newly described.

The smaller room,

containing articles from Christian VI, has been arranged during the present day, and is hung with gold-figured leather; its floor is of peculiarly beautiful inlaid woods of divers colours, and the ceiling is decorated with a beautiful painting Apollo and the muses.

The furniture: Two long mirrors with carved and gilded frames and console-tables belonging to them. — A sofa and many stools with gold-brocate furniture. Two gilded armchairs with green silk covers and decorated with gold fringes. — A cabinet, made in 1735 and paid for, according to tradition, with 1000 gold ducats. Behind the doors of the cabinet, which are furnished both outside and in with mirrors, are three rows of drawers richly inlaid On the pressure of a spring on each of the inner sides of the cabinet a long row of small secret drawers start open. The under portion of the furniture is also rich in inlaid drawers &c. In the uppermost drawer under the leaf is found a harpsichord, which must now be regarded as a great curiosity.

A black japanned toilet table with desk, upon which stands a toilet glass. — A small chest of drawers painted white and ornamented with gilding.

Upon this stands a vase about an ell and a half, representing the element of water.

This is one of the latest works of Magnus Berg; after he had occupied himself with it during more than 12 years death surprised him before he had put the finishing hand to it; at the request of Christian VI, to whom it had been bequeathed by the

Christian VI's smaller room.

The vase of Magnus Berg.

artist's will, it was therefore completed by the renowned painter and curator of the art-chamber J. S. Wahl. On the top above a glass-dome a swan swims in a musselshell; under the cupola we see in magnificent carved work the expedition of Galatæa over the sea. On the spherical surface of the principal piece are in basrelief Neptune, Galatæa, Polyphemus, Europa, Acis and Galatæa, whilst its more exterior surroundings (handles &c.) are formed of dolphins, néreides and water-spouting tritons. The pedestal is formed of 4 dolphins, who from each corner spout water into a musselshell. These as well as the néreides and tritons are formed of silver and ivory alternately. The middle part of the vase is ivory, bound above and beneath by richly gilded, chased and embossed silver work; the band also, that runs over the cupola to bear the swan, is of silver gilt in the form of fruits and leaves.

Upon the console-tables: Two silver vases, lined with mother of pearl and ornamented by cut stones and cameos.

Before the window: A little tastefully finished chandelier of amber with many branches.

In the closet by the window: Two dresses, 1, the coronation dress of Chr. VI (the upper one); 2, his wedding-garments (7th of August 1721). The last named, which is exceedingly well preserved, is the most costly of all the dresses in Rosenborg, being as overloaded with magnificence as aught that the wildest rococo taste could devise. The dark brown material, that forms the ground work of the dress, almost wholly disappears under interwoven silk bouquets, whilst these again are oppressed by a thick layer of gold embroidery sewed upon the dress, so that it has acquired a stiffness and weight, that must have rendered it extremely difficult to wear.

We further find in this closet many guns (6) and pistols (4), that have belonged to Christian VI.

Over the doors: Two excellent embroideries of gold, silver and silk; the one the escutcheon of Denmark and Brandenburgh-Kulmbach, the other a travelling satchel (has belonged to Sophia Magdalena).

In the window: A terra-cotta bust of Christian VI.

The larger room

is covered with hautelisse-tapestry; it has a ceiling-painting (by Coiffre: Flora casting her blessing over Denmark) and a floor of beautiful oak parquetry. We find here a collection of furniture, that in the highest degree deserves attention, since much of it, by reason of its magnificence, as well as of the art and skill expended upon it, and also its more or less bizzarre character, gives a faithful reflection of the taste of the period.

Two cabinets: 1, the one rests upon a carved gilded pedestal; the rest of the piece is also excessively ornamented with carving and rich inlayings of mother of pearl and metal. On the door in the centre of the cabinet, and upon the drawers on both sides, we see, on the first: Christian VI, and on the last: the arms of the provinces. — 2, The other is the work of that skilful cabinet-maker Lehmann, who won his celebrity by furnishing Christiansborg castle, which was so magnificently constructed under Christian VI. This is a very large cabinet, the most striking peculiarity of which is a total destitution of straight lines; drawers, doors — all is curve. It is veneered and ornamented with plateglass, metal &c.

These pieces most excellently characterise the excesses of the rococo style (the decadence): they show what difficulties industry in union with great talent has often been able to overcome, but at the same time how little regard they paid to suitability for the purpose, how often with pains and toil they brought their far-fetched ideas from sources alien to the nature and qualities of the object, instead of employing such as simply and naturally presented themselves.

A turning-lathe in the form of a sort of scrutoire; it belonged to queen Sophia Magdalena. The metal work, wheels &c., very delicately executed, as well as the whole fitting up (it is lined interiorly with red silk) entitle it fully to a place in the workroom of a queen.

Of the furniture to be further named are 4 gilded armchairs, two of them covered with beautiful, well preserved embroidery. — Two chests of drawers with gilded mountings and stone-tops. — On the last named two toilet-glasses with gilded metal frames and a pair of altar candlesticks of silver with the gilded monogram of Christian VI and Sophia Magdalena; were presented to the church of the Orphan asylum by the royal pair; further, a pair of branch candlesticks of silvergilt, each for four lights.

Upon the wall above the chests of drawers: Two timepieces of ebony and silver upon rich stands of the same.

A long mirror, the frame carved and gilded &c.

6

Lehmann's cabinet.

Portraits: 1 portrait of Christian VI (by Wahl); 3 portraits of different sizes of Sophia Magdalena; 2 portraits of their children, prince Frederik and princess Louise; a portrait of the princess Charlotta Amalia (the sister of Christian VI).

In one of the windows: A beautiful marble bust of Christian VI, executed by Jens Carlebye. The pedestal is also of marble with gold decorations; on the front is the kings motto: Deo et populo, to the left and right the dates of his birth and death.

In the other window: The models of two ships of the line, of 70 guns each; the hulls of mother of pearl, amber and tortoise-shell, the rigging of white horse-hair. The one, the Elephant, is 6 inches long and 6 high; it is borne by a merman and a mermaid; the other, 7 inches long and 7 inches high, is raised upon the gilded heads of a merman and a mermaid and some sea animals; an amber-boat with 6 men belongs to the last named ship. They are both the work of a custom-house officier under Christian VI, called Niels Nielsen, of Aalborg (Jutland).

In the corner of the window on a gilded wooden bracket: A tureen-shaped silver wine-cooler and over this a machine with a cover (that ends in a dolphin). Both of them bear the Danish escutcheon in front.

In the corner cupboard by the window: A rich collection of small objects of different agates, marble, heliotrope, onyx, jasper, hornstone &c. Notice particularly a large oblong agate bowl resting upon a foot of silver gilt (a merman with a swan). On the rear of the bowl itself is a representation of the Expedition of Galatæa over the sea in raised work of silver gilt.

Upon the turning-lathe: Under shades 1, An ivory cup, 10 inches high (Sophia Magdalena's work?), 2, The bust of Sophia Magdalena, surrounded by 5 spiral turned pillars, that support a cupola (turned by landgrave William of Hesse).

Over the turning-lathe: 6 figures in ivory and wood. Forming probably 2 groups, a man, woman and child in each. These pieces resemble perfectly in character and execution some work of the same kind in Munnich and Dresden, that date from the inventor of this kind of work (5: the blending of ivory, wood and coloured gems) Simon, born in Hiedhausen near Munnich in the reign of Maximilian III, and it is therefore natural to suppose, that our pieces are also the work of the aboved named artist.

Over the door of egress: A little fowling-piece, the stock of which is covered with green velvet; it belonged to queen Sophia Magdalena. — The antlers of 2 stags, the lower being those of a hart shot by Sophia Magdalena, which feat (according to an uncertain tradition) occasioned the erection of the magnificent palace of Hirschholm.

The palace of Hirschholm was erected between the years 1733—1744. Every resource of art and beauty was called upon to gratify the splendour-loving queen in the construction of this palace, and that the endeavours succeeded in part is proved by the fact, that the knights-hall there is considered as scarcely second to Louis XIV's own magnificent saloons. Christian VI died in this palace and his two immediate successors frequently resided here. Frederik VI suffered the palace to fall into ruins during the years 1810—1812.

In the glass jewel-case: A quantity of ornaments of immense value, watches &c., which Sophia Magdalena in her will (October 10th 1747) decided should be preserved in Rosenborg:

A gold casket with Rose-diamonds presented to her by Christian VI on their marriage 1721. — A pin with the portrait of Christian VI under a diamond. — Another with a magnificent round sapphire, given her by Frederik IV. — Another with an unusually beautiful emerald, cut by Sophia Magdalena's sister, the princess Sophia. — A >green< watch (jasper) with rubies and brilliants, presented to her by Christian VI when once he lay sick in Altona. — A watch with lapis lazuli and brilliants. — Two pairs of heavy diamond ear rings. — An amber box with a little portrait of Christian VI in the middle. — One of agate with brilliants &c. — Another of jasper with rubies and brilliants. — Further a multitude of seals (33) of cornelian, chalcedony, rock-crystal &c. — A key of forged iron, beautifully wrought, used by Christian VI himself upon the palace of Christiansborg.

An example of the order L'Union parfaite«.

Instituted by Sophia Magdalena upon her 11th wedding-day Aug. 7th 1732 to shed lustre on her union with king Christian VI. It was never conferred upon anyone after the death of the founderess. The badge of the order was a white enamelled cross with a gold crown in each of the four ends. Between the arms of the cross were placed alternately the Norwegian lion, with the curved halbard in gold, the handle white enamel, and the Brandenburg eagle, likewise of gold, the wings of red enamel. On the front of the cross in the centre an oval star with rose diamonds and the monograms of Christian VI and Sophia Magdalena in gold upon a blue enamel ground. Behind we read upon a blue enamelled shield: In felicissimæ unionis memoriam·. The order was borne in a blue silk bow with a silver edge.

An enamelled badge of the order of the elephant, borne by Christian VI.

In the two corner cupboards in the east wall: a series of objects of embossed and gilded silver. Part of which belonged to Louise, the daughter of Christian VI (who was married to duke Ernst of Saxe Hildburghausen) whilst another part has been bought in our own day by Christian VIII on Serridslevgaard near Horsens (Jutland).

·L'Union parfaite·.

Let us however particularly notice in this cupboard: A large chalice, cup and paten &c. with the Danish arms, the monogram of Christian VI and the date 1742. Was used by the king in his last days.

The Hirschholm goblet of silver gilt, 22 inches high, which according to tradition has served as a circulating-cup at the dinner table in Hirschholm, for which reason it has always been called Hirscholm's Welcome. The principal part is a bowl, that by six curvatures forms a couch for as many silver gilt cups and which rests upon the head and one arm of a figure, who holds in the other a cornu-copiæ. Rising from the midst of the bowl is a hallow tube, that supports a reservoir for wine in the form of a pine-apple. Upon the tube are three taps (dolphins), by turning which the wine flows from the reservoir through conduits, that run between the curvatures before mentioned, and falls in a jet into the cup of the guest.

In the closet in the principal wall:

A quantity of Japanese porcelain belonging to a large set that came here under Christian VI. — Three silver cups (one of which has 4 Dutch and an imperial medallion as well as a Danish one in the cover, on the occasion of the birth day of Frederik V).

Many glass goblets with the portraits and monograms of Christian VI and his queen cut and gilded upon them. — A glass wine cask. -- A trowel of silver with an ebony handle, used by Christian VI in laying the foundation-stone of Christiansborg (it was also afterwards used in laying the foundation of the town-hall and of St. Johannes Church).

«The Hirschholm goblet».

Frederik IV had expended vast sums upon changes in the castle of Copenhagen, so rich in memories, so as to adapt it to the requirements of the age, but a couple of years afterwards all must fall to gratify the wishes of Sophia Magdalena. In its place arose between 1733—40, seated upon 10,000 piles driven into the ground, that immense castle, which took the name of its new founder and was to have become one of the most magnificent in Europe, but too soon fell a victim to fire (Febr. 26th 1794).

A pyramid-shaped gold-inkstand with the monogram of Christian VI. — A tortoise-shell coffer with inlaying of gold and mother of pearl, on silver gilt feet. There are 6 cut glass bottles, 2 cups, 2 spoons and a sugar-basin of tortoise-shell belonging to it. — A model in silver of the landing-quay at Bergen (the »triangle«) with the triumphal arch erected over it on the visit of Christian VI and his queen to that town Aug. 12th 1733, executed by a goldsmith of Bergen, Johannes Müller. — A small cabinet of silver filigree, finished with extraordinary delicacy, fitted with drawers, the regalia &c., by the same artist. — Many objects of silver-gilt (a can, cups &c.) ornamented by delicately executed drawings in enamel. — A rich collection of objects in amber, many of them of considerable size and others of beautiful and artistic work; as regards the last, notice above all a small man-of-war, four inches long and four and a half inches high. It is an exact model of the ship of the line »Anna Sophia; the artists name was Dietrich de Thura. With regard to work and material this belongs to the most excellent of its kind.

Christian VI died August 6te 1746.

The time of Frederik V (1746—1766).

Scarcely were the eyes of king Christian VI closed before the whole uncomfortable and oppressive feeling, which as a nightmare had weighed upon the minds of the people, dispersed like mist. Never has Denmark seen upon its throne a more sociable king and queen than Frederik V and Louise (daughter of George II of England, born 1724). The oppressive barrier, that until now had separated king and people, was cast down, the gaiety and amusements of the people were no longer sin, and the Danish language was no more too unrefined to be uttered in the highest saloons. This conduct of the young princely pair won from the people a rich measure of affection, which showed itself on many occasions, but most strikingly in the deep sorrow, that seized on every heart, high and low, on the sudden death of queen Louise 1751.

But to all this good nature and natural amiability in Frederik V was united great weakness of character, and — in complete opposition to his industrious father — such a distaste for all serious employment, that so far as respects the government of the state it was happy for the country, that he had by his side such men as Schulin, O. Thott &c., but above all John Hartvig Ernest Bernstorff (born 1712, died 1772). His sincere and most influential

Frederik V.

friend Adam Gotlob Moltke (to whom in 1750 he presented Bregentved as a count's estate) sought early and late to avert from the king personally the unfortunate consequences of his weak character, but unhappily not always with success.

Shortly after the death of his first queen he married Juliana Maria of Brunswick (born 1729, died 1796). —

The objects from the time of this king are now found in one of the rooms that from 1781 to 1868 was used as a cabinet of coins, namely

the south-east corner-room.

This is reached by a passage that runs from the Rose along the east side; it has a flagged floor and the walls are covered with woven tapestry, that dates from about the beginning of the last century. Here we find portraits of Ernst duke of Saxe-Hildburghausen and his consort Louise, sister of Frederik V; princess Charlotta Amalia, daughter of Frederik IV; princess Sophia Carolina of East-Friesland; the Norwegian poet Tullin; the two curators of the art-chamber Morell and L. Spengler; the Danish painter Wahl and the Swedish painter Pilo; the court-architect Laurits Thura; the sculptor Wiedewelt; the statesmen Ivar Rosenkrants and Holstein Lethraborg; the courtfool Kyhl and the Norwegian Drackenberg (born 1626, died 1772). — Further a bronzed gypsum bust of Frederik V and two marble busts: the one Countess Schulin (by an Italian artist Cavaceppi, an admirably executed and intellectually conceived work) the other, Bernstorff, by Wiedewelt.

Frederik V's room is covered with tapestry of red plush flowers upon a yellow silkground; the red colour prevails in the decoration of the walls; the floor is of parquetted oak, the ceiling panelled and painted white and gold.

Of the pictures hung here the most striking are: A large portrait of Frederik V; 6 smaller ones of the king, amongst them two allegorical. One of these represents the genius of painting calling upon Frederik V for protection; it is painted by the well known court-painter Peder Als (born 1725, died 1775), who was the first, who won the great gold medal of the Academy (the Academy of Arts was founded by Frederik V March 31st 1754). — 2 portraits of queen Louise (the larger painted by Pilo). — 2 of queen Juliana Maria. — A portrait of J. H. E. Bernstorff. — The hereditary prince Frederik. — Further: nine coloured crayons representing uniforms from 1757. A margrave of Baireuth;

general count St. Germain; a miniature of privy-councillor Otto
Thott; privy-councillor Hjelmstjerne; the same at 18 years of age;
Bolle Villum Luxdorf and wife. A number of miniatures (33 col-
lected under glass within two principal frames). — Lastly remark
here three busts: Frederik V (in burnt clay); the hereditary prince
Frederik (in gypsum), and count Adam Gotlob Moltke (in delf).

Of the furniture notice: A sofa and many armchairs, gilded
and covered with bluish grey silk, that is decorated with rich
embroidery in silk. — Before the sofa is a writing-table of gilded
wood with a dark grey marble slab, said to have been used by
queen Carolina Mathilde. — Three cabinets ornamented with
gilding and plate glass &c. — A square mirror set in an amber
frame. — A chandelier of amber executed by L. Spengler, after
a design by M. Tuscher (who died 1751).

A timepiece whose chief material is ivory, in the excessive
decoration of which is employed ebony, gilded metal, crystal &c.
This piece, that bears the form of a temple in its principal
characteristic, is a perfect expression of the taste of that time:
the same mixture of motive, brought from the antique and the
rococo, which we meet over all — Corinthian columns, that bound
flats, which are burdened with modern ornaments in raised gilded
work: fruits, the attributs of painting, angels' heads, shells, mussel-
shells ad infinitum. — In spite of this, like some other similar
productions of this period, it is undoubtedly not without a certain
striking effect; nevertheless such an unnatural and unmeaning
blending of different styles must at lenght lead to an opposition,
which, as we shall soon see, in its zeal for right, led to the very
opposite extreme.

In the wardrobe: Two dresses, many weapons &c.

1, the bridal dress of Frederik V (1743), coat, waistcoat,
trowsers (of a white material, inwoven with silver and a rich gold
embroidery) and gold embroidered stockings perfect in themselves
and well preserved.

2, A coat of crimson cloth with richly folded skirts,
immense cuffs and pouch-pockets upon the sides. It is trimmed
with a garniture of broad heavy gold galoon upon the seams,
pockets, cuffs and between the folds of the skirts. The waistcoat
is of white figured silk and likewise edged with goldgaloon.
Frederik V wore this dress once in 1750, when he was present
at the proof of a newly invented cannon in Amager. Through a
want of care two barrels of gun powder took fire and with 62
bombs blew up into the air. As we can imagine this did not

A timepiece.

take place without death and destruction, and the life of the king was in the most obvious peril, from which he was only preserved by the boldness and presence of mind of four cadets. The joy of the metropolis at the preservation of their king was indiscribable. As a remembrance of this day the dress, he had worn, was laid by and preserved.

Two swords with gilded hilts. — Many fire-arms, amongst which a brace of magnificent pistols about 3 quarters long.

The barrels are covered with gold in embossed work, the stocks carved and decorated with heavy, engraved gold mountings. The work of the famous armourer and gunsmith Valentin Mar of Copenhagen and presented to the king as a coronation gift by the citizens of the metropolis.

A walking stick (crutch) used by Frederik V while convalescent once, when he had broken his leg.

In three cabinets: Artistically turned and carved work in ivory.

Of this extraordinary rich collection: decoration-pieces, groups, goblets &c. about half are executed by Lorents Spengler (born in Switzerland 1720, died in Copenhagen 1808) who was the teacher of the royal family in the art of turning. That the practice of this art has been a fashion at the Danish court can be seen, amongst other indications, by this, that Frederik V upon his birth days (March 31st) was usually gladdened by the surprise

A pistol with gold mountings.

of a work executed by one of the princely family alone. Of the works of Spengler preserved here we should distinguish two as interesting for the history of the time, namely one, that regards the hundred years jubilée of the absolute power 1760: cowert within a portal, the bust of Frederik V, upon both sides pillars, between which allegorical figures; above two medals with the portrait of Frederik V &c.; over the whole the Norwegian escutcheon. It is a little work with a tasteful (but naturally regarded as a rococo object) employment of the different materials: ivory, ebony, tortoiseshell &c. — and a second work presented to Frederik V 1761 on the occasion of the abolition of hunting with hounds; it is a Diana (12 inches high) who holds a dog in a fine ivory chain &c.

Of the princely works we distinguish amongst others many of queen Louise's (a little spinning-wheel, ½ an inch high, standing upon an open work pedestal of ivory and ebony. Two small chandeliers of ivory; a ·snail-trap· and a Chinese temple, also ivory); of queen Juliana Maria (a round temple of ivory); of the princes William and Carl of Hesse (many goblets) &c.

By the balcony-window:

A little carriage drawn by four brown horses in which sits a court-lady. Executed by D. de Thura 1749.

In the closet to the right:

A collection of excellent glasswork, amongst which 6 goblets, many of them adorned by carving (the monograms of Frederik V and queen Louise, the Danish arms &c.) executed in Norway; a glascup with a cover with the name of Frederik ·V· and the arms of the Danish provinces in carving and gilding. — A gold coffee set, a present to Frederik V from count Moltke, of whom we have before spoken; they are distinguished by beauty of form and a particularly tasteful engraving of the ornaments; they are Copenhagen work. — A wery large and clear Bohemian topas, on which is cut the bust of Frederik V. This excellent work is from the hand of the renowned lapidary and medallist Joh. Lor. Natter, born in Biberach 1705, died in Petersburg 1763. Christian VI invited him to Denmark and he executed many remarkable works for this king; in 1762 he went to Russia.

A sun-dial with a calendarium perpetuum.

All the ornaments on this piece bear allusion to events, which had taken place in the house of Oldenburg; it was designed and executed by a goldsmith of Copenhagen called Holm and presented by him to Frederik V on the occasion of the 300 years festival of the royal house (1748).

A magnificent badge of the order of the elephant, set with diamonds, rubies and sapphires and the monogram of Frederik V in brilliants. As far as regards the cutting of the stones this is a little chef d'oevre.

A Russian order of St. Andrew in brilliants. According to tradition Catharina II sent this to Frederik V after the death of the Czar Peter III in 1762, who was the deadly enemy of Denmark, as a proof of her desire that peace and friendship should reign again between the two lands.

Two bowls in blue enamel and gilded with covers and plates of silver. On the one of these there is 25 portraits of the ducal family in Brunswick, cut in elaolite by the engraver Bauert, and upon the other 29 copies of antiques in bisquit-paste.

A large collection (88 in number) of precious stones, crystals &c., set in rings, collected by Frederik V. — A collection (13) of seals of crystal, cornelian &c., some of which are set in gold, others on the contrary without any setting; they are admirably carved. — 2 small busts of Frederik V and Juliana Maria. — A gold watch on the face of which in a circle round it are the 12 Oldenborg kings Christian I—Frederik V. — Another with open work behind, through which is seen a ground of agate (it has belonged to Jul. Maria). — A smooth silver watch with the portrait of a lady upon the face. — Two gilded cases, one engraved, the other in addition has open work. — 3 enamelled do., with the portrait of Juliana Maria on two and that of Frederik V on the third. — An ivory tablet in a case, on one side of which is the portrait of Juliana Maria on the other that of the crown-prince Frederik, with a dedicatory inscription written in her own hand from Juliana Maria (to Guldberg). Two engraved gold boxes with blue enamelled lids, on which is the portrait of queen Louise. — A gold box with a lid of mother of pearl, on which is carved a medallion with the first 12 Oldenborg monarchs. — Another the lid of which is of Icelandic obsidian, whereon is carved the portrait of Frederik V. — An amber box carved in relievo (on the lid are the escutcheons of Denmark and England &c.). — A round enamelled gold box; upon the lid the doves of the Capitoline (presented to Jul. Maria by Catharina II, who had herself used it). — A round ivory box with a transparent impression of a ducat in amber on the lid; turned by Frederik V. — 2 enamelled gold boxes with the portraits of the two sons of

Frederik V inside the lids &c. — 3 plain gold rings, two of which were the wedding rings of Frederik V and Juliana Maria; in the third we read: »Der Herr hat alles wohl gemacht« 18 April 1763. — A gold ring, upon the blue ground of the collet under glass the monogram of Juliana Maria. — Another with the monogram of Catharina II upon the collet. — Another with the portrait of Frederik V. — A quantity of Saxon porcelain. — 7 pieces of the oldest Danish porcelain: 3 bowls, in part with lids, and 4 small mugs with covers; the colour of some is green, of others blue.

These interesting pieces date from the time of Frenchman Fournier. This man, as is well known, founded in the reign of Frederik V, a porcelain factory by »Blaataarn«; it had not however any long existence, since the undertaking, as he conducted, required from the state by far too large and inordinate contributions. However, as can be seen from the last mentioned articles, the manufactory produced very excellent object during the few years it existed, which was certainly owing as much to the admirable assistance he received from the skilful artists Ruch, Seipsius and Gylding, all painters.

Amongst the works of the last named artist from Fourniers time we see to left a finely executed porcelain painting: In the midst Christ, who with bound hands is led before Pilate, surrounded by the apostles.

How zealous of his honour this artist must have been, is shown by the tradition of his death, which is said to have been caused by sorrow at the springing, in the burning of a plate, on which was painted in enamel a picture of Frederik V as the patron of arts and sciences.

Frederik V died Jan. 14th 1766.

From the time of Christian VII (1766—1808).

In the year when Christian VII ascended the throne, being 17 years old, he married the princess Carolina Mathilde, the sister of George III, king of England. During a journey, he made abroad in 1768, he made acquaintance with Joh. Friedrich Struensee, whom he constituted his private physician and who in a short time succeeded in winning his highest favour. After his return to Denmark Struensee rose from one post of honour to another, and having also succeeded in gaining the affection of the young queen and when by degrees the king, debilitated by early dissipation,

Christian VII.

became infirm of intellect, he stood alone at the helm of state with, one can say, the whole sovereign power in his own hand. Sorrowfully and abruptly was this dominion ended by the decapitation of himself and his friend Brandt, the divorse of the queen and her consequent exile, where in the course of a few years she died in Celle (Maj 10th 1775).

Struensee's ministry was succeeded by that of Guldberg, which in opposition to it was animated by a warm feeling of Danish nationality, but in many directions wanted its free spirit, and it had in particular no eye for that great and vital question for Denmark: the freedom of the peasantry. This great act was reserved for the successor of Guldberg's ministry (the younger Bernstorff and his noble assistants) who was interpreter for the young warm-hearted prince, who in 1784 seized the helm of the state himself and held it uninterruptedly in his hand for 55 years, although in 1808 he was first called Frederik VI. Commerce flourished (particularly during the American war of freedom), and from this flowed wealth and prosperity, the freedom of peasantry &c. All these circumstances made a great portion of Christian VII's reign a period of happiness for Denmark — then came the French revolution, that inaugurated a new period with storms: the bright and quiet days preceding it were but the calm of the ocean, that precedes the tempest.

We shall make acquaintance with the period of Christian VII by the side of the room of Frederik V in

the south-west corner-room,

which is decorated exactly as the foregoing, with the exception of the floor, that is painted grey.

Upon the walls we see: 6 portraits of Christian VII (3 of which are painted by Jens Juel, born 1745, died 1801; the largest represents the king in his coronation robes with the regalia). — 7 portraits of queen Carolina Mathilda. — The queen dowager Juliana Maria. — The hereditary prince Frederik. — 3 portraits of the crown-prince Frederik (2 as a child). 2 portraits of princess Louise Augusta (the one as a child). — 3 portraits of Struensee. — Count Enevold Brandt. General Eickstedt. — Andreas Peter Bernstorff. — 13 small miniatures viz: the kings of the house of Oldenborg to Christian VII (collected within one frame under glass upon a yellow ground). — A miniature half-length portrait of the hereditary prince Frederik, painted by Høier.

— 15 miniatures (collected in one frame) namely: Christian VII (6); Carolina Mathilda (2); Juliana Maria; Louise Augusta (2); the hereditary prince Frederik; the crown-prince Frederik (2) &c. — Still further 2 drawings by Captain W. Haffner »An evening party at the court in Christiansborg palace 1781«, which contains a number of portraits: the royal family, the minister Guldberg, the foreign ambassadors &c. — A marble bust of A. P. Bernstorff by Dajon (born 1748. died 1824). — A gypsum bust of Juliana Maria. – A metal bust (black with gold) of the afterwards king Frederik VI as a child.

In the bay window:

A large timepiece ornamented with painting, gilding, cut glass &c. — A cane walking-stick with a gold top, on which is engraved the name of Struensee.

Under the ceiling:

A clock in form of a gilded birdcage: the dial is turned downwards.

Upon one of the tables:

An artistic work in ivory, 36 inches high, executed in 1782 by the ivory-turner J. C. Opitz. (Under a pyramid-shaped glass shade.)

The furniture here consists of tables (3), chairs, mirrors, sconces &c., in which the straight lines begin to be prominent, and presents a very interesting contribution to the knowledge of the chief characteristic of the style, that prevailed towards the period of the great French revolution (the substitute for the decadence), — or, as we may say: of the struggle for the reintroduction of the antique simplicity.

In the closet between the windows:

A quantity of porcelain, belonging to the ›flora danica‹ set (of which more hereafter). — Many objects in glass: decanters, glasses, goblets. Amongst the last a goblet on the occasion of the marriage of Christian VII and Carolina Mathilda; of which a little Cupid informs os, by the act of scratching with his arrow under the crowned monogram of the bridal pair, engraved in the glass. the following: ›Felici sidere juncti MDCCLXVI d. 8 (i. e. November). On the other side are the Danish and English escutcheons. The cover terminates in a crown with 6 curvatures. The whole is 3 quarters high.

We notice further in this closet: A porcelain statuette of Christian VII. The king is dressed in the Imperial robes, and

A goblet of Christian VII and Carolina Matilda.

leans against a chronological tree of the house of Oldenborg, on which are the portraits of the kings of that house.

In the closet by the entrance-door:

The coronation dress of Christian VII, namely the dress of a Spanish cavalier of a white material with gold, ornamented with heavy gold lace. -- A hunting uniform: blue cloth coat, edged with broad silver and gold galoon, a red cloth waistcoat and knee-breeches together with a hat, a riding whip and a silver mounted hunting knife with an ebony hilt. A present from Louis XV to Christian VII during his stay in Paris. — The wedding dress of Christian VII of silver moiré, trimmed with garlands of flowers, formed of spangles and gold foil. The embroidery upon the sleeve-facings and the waistcoat consists of lines crossing each other with a little ornament in each square, all of gold. — With the dress last named a gala sword with the hilt of gold, richly set with diamonds, which, on an opaque ground, arrange themselves in bouquets and garlands. — A sword with a silver gilt sheath, finished upon Frederiksværk.

In the window to the left:

The diploma of Christian VII as Doctor, from the universities of Oxford and Cambridge together with his letters of freedom as a citizen of London and member of the corporation of goldsmiths of that city.

In the glasscase:

The gold caskets belonging to the letters of freedom, last spoken of, namely: heavy goldboxes with engraven ornaments. --- Rings, amongst which one with the portrait of Carolina Mathilda. — A watch, that together with the broad chain, to which it is attached, is set with brilliants. This extremely costly ornament, which was the property of Carolina Mathilda, belongs to the jewellery, that after the fall of the queen in the year 1773 was transferred from Christiansborg to be preserved in Rosenborg.

2 gold watches, the one set with diamonds, the other with the signet of Christian VII dependent from it. — 2 Norwegian case-knifes. — A portrait in relievo of Christian VII, composed with remarkable skill of diamonds splinters set in silver.

Christian VII died March 13th 1808.

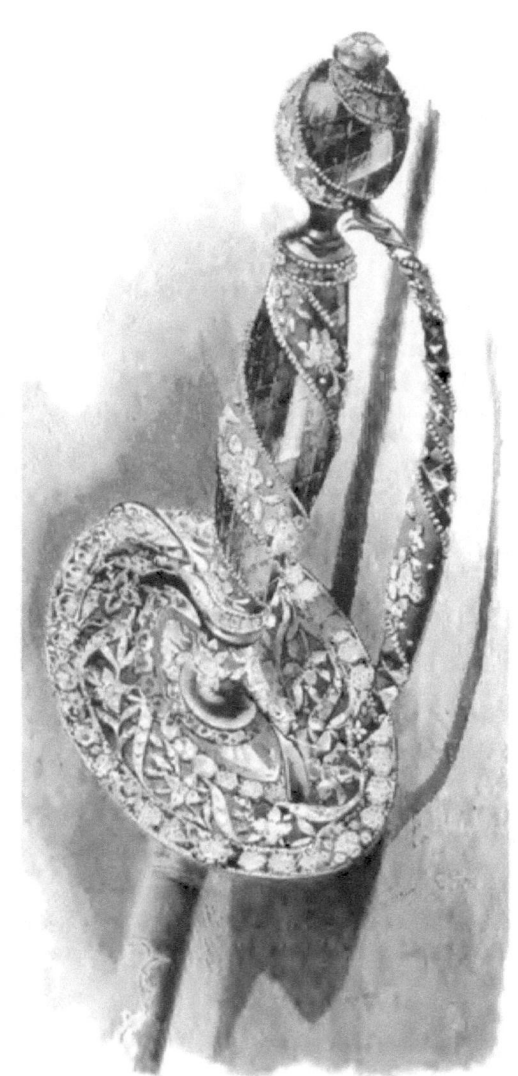

A gala sword of Christian VII.

Frederik VI.

III.

From the French revolution to our own times.

From the time of Frederik VI (1808—1839).

As already alluded to, Frederik VI had for 24 years — since 1784 — been in realty the veritable ruler of the kingdoms of Denmark and Norway when his father died, and the interior social progress as well as the general prosperity and welfare, that mark the greater part of these years, are therefore essentially connected with him. But the happy condition of these days came to an abrupt end: the loss of the fleet (in 1807), the separation of Norway from the monarchy (in 1814), the money-dearth after the war, and many other things exhausted the strength of Denmark for a long time, and it was only to the close of the old kings life that vitality and growth revived again in the paralysed body of the state. He had himself given a powerful impulse towards arousing the people to a freer development, by the introduction in May 1831 of the »raadgivende Provinsialstænder« (provincial assemblies, who had the privilege of debating upon the laws).

In joy as in sorrow, in prosperity as in misfortune Frederik VI was one with the Danish people, and when he died, their sorrow was deep and heartfelt; the peasants bore him to the grave and the beautiful funeral songs, sung for him, will bear his memory far down the streame of time to other generations. His queen was Maria Sophia Frederikka (princess of Hesse-Cassel), born 1767, died March 21st 1852.

Already a long time before the revolution towards the end of the 18th century burst out, the war against the »wigs« had begun in France. The new doctrine of forsaking all artifical modes end returning to the simplicity of nature (Rousseau) had penetrated farther and farther, and as at the same time, by the many discoveries in the newly rediscovered cities of Pompeii and Herculanum, the interest in the antique was reawakened by the increased acquaintance with it, so they found in its forms the expression of what they sought. The new taste was carried upon the wild stream of the revolution around the world, and the first French empire disposed itself to give to these forms a peculiar worth and gravity. Therefore it is, that the reigning style, in buildings, furniture &c., which in the beginning of this century has exchanged the variegated spirals of the rococo for the simple rectangular forms of the antique, has received the name of ›the Imperial renaissance‹.

This style first meets our eye, when from the room of Christian VII we enter that of Frederik VI, which has but one window, that overloaks the drilling-ground. This and the two following rooms, the first of which contains principally the objects from Christian VIII and the second those from Frederik VII, have all under the new arrangement of the collection been painted and decorated, so that each alone is a contribution to the picture of the time of each king concerned. The attention is particularly called to the different decorations of the ceilings.

The furniture in

the room of Frederik VI

is wholly distinguished by its extraordinary simplicity and much of it adapted to illustrate the imperial style in its highest grade. Notice in particular the semi-round buffet opposite the entrance door and the cabinet, that stands by the end wall.

If for example we remember the cabinet before described of Christian VI's time, the ressemblance in many respects between this and that piece of furniture will be striking. In that, spite of all the absurdity and exaggeration expended upon the motive, one could not do other than yield our admiration to the high degree of industry and skill, that was displayed in all, even in the execution of the most insignificant parts — here: the artificial is certainly most distant and simplicity is called forth, but if we only remark, for ex: how disproportionately the pillars are employed as ornaments (do but peep within the small doors of the cabinet and remark its more than economically furnished interior), we shall perceive without difficulty, that this was never the course taken by the antique in its endeavours after simplicity and nature.

The room of Frederik VI.

A deal-desk, painted white, the leaf covered with green cloth, which together with many of the objects, that stand upon it (inkstand &c.), has been used by Frederik VI.

On both sides of the entrance to the room of Christian VIII:

Two gueridons, upon each of which a candelabrum in the form of a vase stands, from which the branches (of gilded metal) issue as flowers. — A small table with an oval slab of metal; upon this stands a model of a ship of the line of 116 guns, fabricated by some of the Danish prisoners of war in England, of bones procured at their meals.

In the window: A coffee set of Copenhagen porcelain (coffee pot, four cups and saucers &c.) white and gold; they have belonged to Frederik VI.

Upon the buffet: A silver goblet with a cover. It bears the coins of the Swedish minister Görtz (after the death of Charles XII) and an inscription in reference to the campagn i Sweden in 1788.

Portraits:

A large picture, containing the portraits of Frederik VI and queen Maria with their two daugthers (by Eckersberg). — 7 portraits of Frederik VI of different sizes (4 painted, 1 in relievo in ivory, 1 drawn with silver pencil upon parchment (by Grøger) an 1 a medallion portrait in drawing). — His bronzed gypsum bust; his equestrian statuette in ivory upon a tortoiseshell pedestal. — 3 portraits of queen Maria (the one by Juel). — The princess Sophia Frederikka (the mother of Christian VIII). — Christian VIII as prince. — A gypsum bust of princess Carolina Amalia. — The hereditary prince Ferdinand. His wife, the hereditary princess Carolina. — Princess Louisa Augusta (Frederik VI's sister), a full sized portrait. Frederik VI and queen Maria driving to the theatre by torch-light.

Abowe the wardrobe: A quantity of porcelain belonging in part to the flora danica set.

Weapons: A little foil, used by Frederik VI as a boy; an infantry musket with a bayonet (his drill weapon as a young prince); 2 pistols; a Turkish sword with a red velvet scabbard &c.

In the wardrobe: Dresses: Many uniforms, amongst which the regimentals of Frederik VI with the badge of honour of a Dannebrog's-man fastened upon the coat. — The coronation robes of Frederik VI. — The robes of the orders of the elephant and the garter, belonging to Frederik VI, &c.

The Dannebrog order, to which we have alluded above, was renewed by Christian V (the day after his son's birth October 12th 1671), but nevertheless its first creation dates back to the days of Valdemar »Seir« (the victorious) and the renowned Volmer-battle (1219) in which »the Dannebrog« (the national standard of Denmark) fell down from heaven. The 35 heroes, on whom after the battle the king conferred knighthood under the shadow of the newly-fallen banner of the cross, are regarded as the first knights of the Dannebroge. Christian V, as we have said, renewed the order, when in honour of the birth of the crown-prince he named 19 knights. The statutes, given by him, are dated December 1st 1693. According to these there was only one grade (the white knight«), the order could be conferred only upon the nobility, and was so restricted, that its numbers could not at any one time surpass 50. Frederik VI Juni 28th 1808 changed the order, en-creasing the grades to four (grand commander, grand cross, com-mander and knight) and extending the admission to commoners. At the same time he instituted the silver cross, i. e. the badge of the Dannebrog's-men, which can be bestowed upon those also, who are already received in one or other of the grades of the parent order, equally with others. Under Frederik VII the grade of commander was still further extended and divided into two grades, the 1st and 2nd.

The room of Christian VIII

contains still from the time of Frederik VI: much furniture; sofa, chairs (white and gold, with covers of green silk); a large round deal-table, very simple, used by Frederik VI for his privy-council table. — In the glasscase upon it: his diploma as a knight of the garter (1822) with the statutes and the seal, appending in a gilded capsule. — The silver travelling-watch of Frederik VI. A pedo-meter (used when exercising). — The decorations of a number of foreign orders.

Amongst these 3, that no longer exist: the French order of the Holy Ghost; the Dutch order of Union (Louis Bonaparte) and the Westphalian Crown order (Jerome Bonaparte); these on the death of the king could not be returned, since the respective dynasties, by whom they were bestowed, had ceased to exist.

Frederik VI died December 3rd 1839.

From the time of Christian VIII (1839—1848).

King Christian VIII, born Sept. 18th 1786, was married to his first wife Charlotta Frederikka of Mecklenburgh-Schwerin Juni 21st 1806, from whom he was separated 1809. On the 22nd May 1815 he was the second time married with the present queen dowager Carolina Amalia, daughter of duke Frederik Christian of Augustenborg.

The principal interest to note in the furniture in Christian VIII's room is the difference in the material from that of the foregoing periods, the gilded wood having now given place to mahogny. For the rest is most prominent:

Upon the walls: the portraits:

Christian VIII (3). Queen Carolina Amalia (3). The grand-duke Friederich Franz of Mecklenburg Schwerin (died 1837). His consort Louise (died 1808). The princess Wilhelmina (the present duchess of Glücksburg). The landgrave William of Hesse Cassel (the father of our present queen, born 1787, died 1867). Frederik VI lying in state. 2 paintings and 2 drawings (by Gertner), represen-ting the anointment and coronation of Christian VIII and Carolina Amalia in the chapel of Frederiksborg castle Juny 28th 1840. Christian VIII lying in state and castrum doloris. The sculptor Thorvaldsen and the poets Oehlenschläger and Ingemann. The natural philosopher H. C. Ørsted.

On the table under the four last:

The magnificent drinking-horn of gold, richly ornamented with precious stones and allegorical figures in embossed and engraved work, presented to the poet Ingemann by the Danish ladies on the occasion of the feast, in celebration of his 70th birth day in Sorø, May 28th 1859.

In the closet remark:

Dresses: the magnificent coronation dress of Christian VIII. — A dress of red velvet, worn by the king at the opening of the High Court of Justice. — The robes of the order of the elephant. — Many uniforms &c.

Before the constitution of Juny 5th 1849 the monarch himself was by right the president in the supreme court, and as such presided at the opening of the court until 1848 on the first monday in every month of March.

Christian VIII.

Still further we find on the base of the closet amongst other things:

Some models for muskets. — A carved wooden jug with a lid (presented to Christian Frederik (Christian VIII) during his recidence in Norway as elected king 1814). An ivory bust of Christian VIII. — A goblet and a box with cover, of ivory; the last named objects are works of the present school of art in Denmark as well as some small plastic works, the figures of animals in ivory &c. upon two of the tables.

Lastly we find in the glass-case:

A chamberlain's key, with the monogram of Christian Frederik the later Christian VIII — (from the period of his residence in Norway as elected king 1814). — A couple of foreign orders, born by Christian VIII. — A gilded hammer, used by Christian VIII at the presentation of new colours to the army to strike the nails in the staffs. The diploma of Christian VIII as Dr. juris from the university of Oxford in a gold capsule. — His own gold watch and two gold watches with enamelled portraits (at the back of one Christian VIII's and on the other that of the crown-princess Carolina Mariana). — A couple of favourite porcelain cups, gilded, with the names Charlotta and Frederik (his first consort and their son). — The medicine spoon he used upon his death-bed.

Christian VIII died Jan. 20th 1848.

From Christian VIII's we enter lastly into

the room of Frederik VII,

which is lighted from a single window and decorated in the Frederiksborg-style , which as is well known was much favoured by Frederik VII and his contemporaines.

From the time of Frederik VII (1848—1863).

King Frederik VII, born October 6th 1808, was three times married, first with the princess Wilhelmina, daughter of Frederik VI, next with Carolina Mariana of Mecklenburg-Strelitz, both these marriages ended in divorse. In 1850 he contracted a morganatic marriage with countess Danner. — On the 5th of Juny 1849 he from the plenitude of his sovereign power gratuitously gave to his people a free constitution based on fundamental law.

Frederik VII.

Upon the walls:

Many portraits of Frederik VII as a child and youth (amongst the first an excellent one by Grøger). — A painting by A. Melby: Danish men-of-war, the ship of the line ›Christian VIII‹, the corvette ›Flora‹ and the brig ›Allart‹, saluting for the princess Carolina Charlotta Mariana, that was brought by the steamer ›Kiel‹ to the landing quay by Holmen's church Juni 22nd 1841. — Two paintings of the procession on the castle square. — A large portrait of Frederik VII as king (in admiral's dress, by Gertner). — A relief portrait of the same king in terra cotta (modelled by the medalist Conradsen). — 2 small portraits in relief of him and his consort Mariana, in ivory. — Over the exit door hangs an old picture of Frederiksborg.

Of the furniture we remark particularly:

The writing-table of the king; on which rest his writing materials of gilded metal, amongst which is the pen, he used Juny 5th 1849 to sign the free constitution of Denmark.

Upon the cabinet:

Two large vases of Sèvres china, presented to the king the year before his death by the emperor Napoleon III, and two vases in biscuit (17½ inches high) presented to the collection by Charles XV, king of Sweden and Norway, from the manufactory of Gustafsberg near Stockholm. — Between these the bust of the king Frederik VII in biscuit, executed in the porcelain factory of the brothers Bing after a model by Bissen. — Behind the bust a couple of the king's swords and other weapons.

In the cabinet:

A series of dresses: the Danish and Swedish hussar uniforms of Frederik VII, ornamented with the orders of the three Northern countries; his uniforms as admiral and general; his aluminium's helmet; his robes of the order of the elephant; the crimson gold embroidered fez, used by the king (for ex. in the theatre and at home) &c. — A beautifully finished admiral's rapier, given to Frederik VII by his father, the work of the Danish jeweller Rudolfi, who resided in Paris. — The speaking-trumpet, used by the king on board ship. — A cabin bell-rope (a silver chain with a crystal hand piece), used on board the king's steam yacht ›Falken‹ and which originally belonged to Tordenskjold. — The masonic order of the king. — A large cut glass goblet. — A painted cup and saucer of Copenhagen porcelain (used in travelling). — The silver table-bell of Frederik VII (according to tradition it has formerly been

used by many queens, the last of which was Carolina Mathilda). —
A number of tobacco-pipes, ordinarely used by him. — A multitude of shooting-badges, worn by Frederik VII as member of
different shooting-clubs.

Finely upon the wall we further notice:

The insignia of many of Frederik VII's foreign orders.

In the window:

A model of his yacht Falken«.

Frederik VII died November 15th 1863.

Our progress through the strictly chronological collection being
now fully ended we ascend the spiral staircase — again past a
series of historical portraits: Hans Gram (the celebrated and learned
historian, really the founder of the Danish Scientific Society &c.,
born 1685, died 1748), Luxdorf (a renowned jurist and philosopher,
born 1716, died 1788) and many others — up the third story, and
enter the room, that king Frederik IV in the first quarter of the
last century so magnificently fitted up.

The knight's-hall

This hall, which extends over the entire length and breadth
of the palace, is 150 feet long, including the bay-windows in the
end-wall, its breadth is 28 and the height about 19 feet. Its
present fitting-up as we have said dates from Frederik IV, all that
remains from Christian IV being two marble chimney-pieces at the
ends of the hall (the northern behind the drapery of the throne).

The arched roof rests upon stucco-cornices, that are marbled
by Charles Bracht and which run along the four sides of the hall.
It is ornamented with rich and beautiful relief in stucco. In the
middle is seen the Danish escutcheon (painted in its heraldic
colours, whilst the rest of the work in relief is unpalnted); on both
sides of the concavity under the escutcheon is a lion, which genii
are crowning and which rests in a festooned field; upon the centre
line of the ceiling (right and left of the escutcheon) are four large
paintings by Heinrich Krock, representing the four emblems of
royalty: towards the north »the sword and globe«, to the south
»the crown and scepter«, all borne by genii and allegorical figures.
These pictures have rich stucco mountings of entwined roses, lilies,
laurel and oak leaves and are united by magnificent compartments,
which on each side of the curving spreads out into a royal mantle,
suspended upon the trunk of an elephant; the upper corners of

this mantle are lifted by genii and it forms the back ground of a shield with the crowned monogram of Frederik IV and two recumbent lions as shield-bearers. On both sides of the arched ceiling we see four large representations in relievo of important acts of the government under Frederik IV: that on the south-easterly side: the abolition of villanage, opposite, the institution of the land-militia; on the north-easterly side the institution of the dragoons, and opposite the enrollment of the seamen. Upon the mantel-piece on each side of the throne-canopy and of the chimney-piece on the opposite end-wall we see four allegorical figures of the four quarters of the earth, Europa, America, Asia and Africa; behind them are the four principal winds. — The whole of this work, taken in connection with its time, may in many respects challenge its equal in beauty.

The floor is painted in marble squares and the decoration of the walls is a marbling of strong mixed colours round a series of large historical hautelisse-tapestries, uniting the whole into a highly characteristic picture. Over the entrance-door we see the portrait of Frederik IV in gypsum; straight opposite above the entrance to the room of the Regalia the portrait of Christian V in marble; both these relief-pictures are surrounded by a rich ornamentation of white painted wood and stucco. The tapestry, which was executed in Christian V's time at Kjøge by the Dutch brothers van der Eicken after the designs of the Danish painter Peter Andersen, gives a series of battle-pieces, by sea and land, from the war in Scania (with many veritable portraits). The seafights in particular are most effectively executed, and as regards the study of the dress of that period and the build of the ships &c. these tapestries are invaluable. They are 12 in number, each 12 feet in height, whilst the breadth varies from 10 to 22 feet. The subjects represented are:

1, The taking of Wismar 13th December 1675.
2, The capture of Landscrona castle 4th Aug. 1676.
3, The battle upon Kolbergerheide Juny 1st 1677.
4, The taking of Marstrand 23rd July 1677.
5, The landing on Scania 29th Juny 1676.
6, The seafight by Øland 1st Juny 1676.

Upon the eastern wall from North to South.

1, The taking of Helsingborg 3rd July 1676.
2, The taking of Christiansstad 15th Aug. 1676.
3, The taking of Rygen 17th Sept. 1677.

8*

4, The taking of Damgarten in Pommern 6th Octbr. 1675.

5, The battle in Kjøge-bay 1st July 1677.

6, The taking of Landscrona 11th Juny 1676.

Upon the western wall from South to North.

On each side of the northern fire-place is placed a high mirror with frames and consoles of embossed silver, that were formerly part of the fitting up of Christiansborg. Before the southern fire-place, in which an iron stove has been set, with a drum and the date 1721, we see a screen, also of embossed silver, and two large heatreflectors (balls) of silver, that rest upon iron-dogs (andirons); these date from Christian V's days. Above the chimney-piece is placed a bracket, on which stands a bust of Christian IV in white marble. Amidst the tapestry we find many beautifully cut glasses in red japanned frames, ornamented with silver, and along the side-walls 18 high-backed carved chairs; the embroidery of the seats and back was, according to tradition, sewn by Charlotta Amalia, queen dowager after Christian V, together with her ladies of the bed-chamber, in the years 1699 and 1700, following the marks on the embroidery.

As the hall now appears after the complete restauration, that it has undergone in these times and which was completed in 1869, it stands before us as an excellent architectural memorial from the beginning of the last century. It has however other grounds, on which it presents itself to our notice, in the historical memories, that are associated with it (it was the custom formerly to hold all the royal festivals here, and from 1795—1829 the feast of opening of the Supreme court as well as the solemn investiture of orders were held here &c.) and impart to it a high degree of interest, which is still further increased by the fact, that the knight's-hall is now the depository of a number of objects, still used at the coronation and other solemn occasions. These objects are:

The two coronation-chairs.

They are both of same hight — about 8 feet — and the same form, but with a marked difference as to material and all that regards the fittings up. The king's chair, which is of narwhal-horn, is ornamented by 8 allegorical figures, formed of metal, of which 4 sit in the interior, one by each corner of the seat, 2 stand in recesses above the back supporters and 2 in a recumbent position upon the canopy, whose apex terminates in the globe and cross. Beneath this stand a very large square crystal-spar, which on the day of coronation is replaced by an amethyst of the same size, preserved among the Regalia. The canopy is still further decorated by two oval Mocha-stones, which, according to tradition, are the gift of an Indian prince. In front upon the arm-rests are 2 gilded balls. The upper portion of the arm-rests, the seat and the back are covered with gold brocade.

The queen's chair is smaller than the king's; it is of wood, entirely covered with thick plates of silver, in many places ornamented with gold. On the canopy 2 allegorical figures recline, Piety and Benevolence, whilst between them, from the silver-gilt plate, the name of Jehovah radiates in Hebrew characters. The seat and back are covered with silver brocade.

The want of uniformity between the coronation chairs arises from the circumstance of their having been made at different periods; that of the king was finished for Christian V and the queen's not until the time of Christian VI. The principal material in the king's chair, the narwhal-horn, had at the time it was procured a value equal to its weight in silver (thus says tradition), and as it is very heavy, we can judge how expensive the chair must have been. This chair was first used 1671, the queen's in 1731.

The three silver lions.

They are chased and embossed with gilded manes. Being exceedingly large they possess on that ground alone a considerable value, but the mere worth of the metal vanishes before the surpassingly excellent and unrivalled importance of the work. They recline before the king's throne on the day of coronation and other high solemnities (the opening of the »Rigsdag« ɔ: the Parliament by the king in person) as symbols of the lions in the escutcheon of Denmark.

According to recent inquiry these three lions have probably been executed in Copenhagen, whilst earlier tradition intimated, that they were made in Augsburg.

4 large candalabra and 12 gueridons of silver. Used on solemn occasions (coronations, funerals &c.); dates from the time of Frederik IV and Christian VI.

The Royal font.

It is of silver (weighing 360 oz) and 3 feet high. The breadth across the dish is 2 feet and 9 inches. It is richly adorned with gilding, pictures in embossed work and other ornaments: heads of angels, foliage &c. On the bottom of the dish we see ›the Baptism of Christ‹, upon the margin there are three smaller representations of scriptural subjects. At the time of the baptismal solemnity within this dish is placed another of gold, ordinarily preserved amongst the Regalia and of which we shall speak further.

Regarding the age of this font we know nothing certain. It was sent to Rosenborg for preservation under Frederik IV (October 2nd 1720), and it has always been assigned to this

The Royal font.

monarch's time. It ought however judging from probability to be older, since much of the embossed work especially reminds us of similar work of the time of Frederik III. —

The glass-room.

that lies by the knight's-hall in the north eastern tower, was arranged 1714 by Frederik IV. Its walls are covered with green silk damask and here and there hung with paintings, which however have worth only as decorative pictures; the panels and doors are silvered and adorned with gilt fillets, and on the painted ceiling a bacchanal procession is represented. From the green glass-wall on each side of the entrance door a multitude of shelves spring forth, arranged with great taste and art, and adorned with rich gold edges and garlands of green glass leaves and different coloured glass fruits. On these shelves is found an abundant collection of the elder Venitian glass, which ought perhaps to be esteemed the most excellent of its kind, and which but for its intelligent and tasteful arrangement would be overpowering. First and foremost we must in this respect point out its richess in the renowned filigree- or thread-glass, which is no longer fabricated as before and for this reason, should it chance to be offered for sale, it can scarcely be bought for gold; next the costly ruby-glass; further the imitations of the different precious stones in glass, the sapphire-, emerald-, amethyst- and opal-glass &c. — That which will also particularly awaken the admiration and wonder of the visitors is the great variety, both in form and object, here represented: table-bells, knives, forks and spoons; pots, tankards, cups, flowers, bottles and drinking-glasses &c. ad infinitum. Lastly we pray you to remark the extraordinary beauty of the carving on the particular articles.

The whole of this rare and valuable collection (with the exception of the large covered glass goblets resting on the basement, and also a couple of glasses, which are of Norwegian manufacture), are from the glass and mirror manufactory, so renowned in its time, that was situated on the isle of Murano near Venice, and according to tradition were given by the doge to Frederik IV during his visit there in the beginning of 1709.

The fabrication of glass, the first traces of which we must look for thousands of years ago, without doubt originally dates from the Egyptians. Transplanted from thence to Rome in the time of the emperors it was carried to Byzantine by Constantine the great. About the beginning of the 14th century it was brought from thence to Venice, where it quickly rose to a height previously unknown. To keep the working of the glass masses and the whole artistic method of fabrication as secret as possible, the manufactory was placed in Murano, where it still flourishes, and has taken new expansion since the incorporation of Venice with the kingdom of Italy. The Venitian glass was renowned particularly for its colours, while other glass, the old German e. g. was remarkable for the

application of enamel, engravings &c.   The discoverer of the art
of engraving glass was a German, Caspar Lehmann (1609).

The porcelain-room

lies in the south east tower by the knight's-hall and dates from
the present.   The basis of this collection arose from the quantity
of costly porcelain which was scattered about the castle and con-
siderably added to by presents and in other ways. In this manner
the collection now contains in rich selection excellent specimens
of Japanese, Chinese, French, Saxon and Danish porcelain besides any Swedish articles, partly of old and partly of
modern date, wich, by a dark brownish back-ground, is so set off
that notwithstanding its abundant variety it is easy to inspect.
The whole is so arranged, that standing by the window just'
opposite the entrance door we have upon the left side-wall the
Japanese-chinese department, on the wall just opposite to the left
of the door the French and to the right of the same the Saxon
departments; on the right side-wall and continuing from thence
upon the window-wall to the window the Danish department; and
lastly in the window itself the Swedish articles.   Thus as we see
an historical thread is drawn from left to right.

The Japanese and Chinese articles date particularly from
the time of Christian VI; it is not a large but a rare and costly
collection; the time of its fabrication we have no means of ascer-
taining, but its antiquity is certainly very great.

The Saxon porcelain for the most part dates from Frederik V,
but single specimens are also found here of that brown porphyra-
ceous fabric of the earliest period of the Meissen porcelain now so
rare (Böttger — i. e. before 1709, in which year for the first time
he produced porcelain white and transparent).   The greatest part
of this division has been brought here by the elder Schimmelmann;
it is of extreme beauty and excellence; the ground is white, clear
and even the gold rich and strong, and the landscapes &c., with
which each article however small is adorned, are veritable masterpieces of this kind. '

The French department was brought here under Frederik V
and Christian VII, and belonged in part to the great service that
Christian VII received of Louis XV during his visit to Paris 1768.
It is from the renowned Sèvres manufactory in the period of its
palmiest days.   This was originally a private establishment and
carried on in Vincennes, from which place in 1756 it was removed

to Sèvres, and in 1760 Louis XV undertook the charge of it, and conducted it with passionate ardour; it was supported and helped forward in every way, so that in a short time it produced works that even in the present day are regarded as unapproachable. We here e. g. particularly remark the porcelain paintings (1766): how delicate and yet vigourous in form and delineation are they not! The blue colour of the vases and the rest clear, deep and soft. The gilding as strong and effective as if it were smelted into the objects, and the flower-representations so fresh and warm.

The Danish department is also a beautiful witness of Danish industry in this direction. A great part of it belongs to the renowned »Flora danica« service, which is regarded as so greatly significant that in the resolutions of the Chronological collection it is expressly named as one of its permanent constituents. The origin of this dates from the conclusion of the last century, when — following tradition — it was intended for Russia in accordance with an order of Catherina II, which was withdrawn by the emperor Paul &c. It was bought for account of the state treasure of the manufactury for 10,000 Rd. (20,000 Danish crowns) by order of the prince regent, Januar 2nd 1803, to the lord high steward Hauch. It has a white colour of a rare purity and clearness and each separate piece is adorned with a different example of the Flora of Denmark. The pictures are executed by skilful artists after the work »Flora danica«. — We further find in this division amongst other things several characteristic vases of older times and a magnificent bust in biscuit of the queen dowager Juliana Maria. — All these objects are from the earliest Royal Danish porcelain factory that was established after the druggist J. H. Müller's discovery of porcellain-clay in the neightbourhood of Rønne in the isle of Bornholm (1772). It was first worked by a private company of shareholders, but in 1779 the king undertook the charge of the factory and evidently following in the track of the factory of Meissen soon very much enlarged it. In 1868 it again became private property and has been considerable increased.

(Factory marks for the elder French and Saxon porcelain. 1, In 1753 the French porcelain had two L's twisted together with an a in the middle. Until 1777 the middle letter was continued in alphabetical order, thus: 1753a—1754b &c. From 1777—1793 the middle letter was doubled. Under the republic until 1801 the letters R. F. — 2, The early Saxon porcelain showed the three letters A. R. P. (Augustus Rex Poloniæ) or a rod of Æsculapius, or two drawn swords crossed downwards; after the time of Böttger the swords are crossed upwards.)

The chamber of the Regalia,

which lies by the knight's-hall in the west-tower and is not as a rule open to the public, has also in connection with the new arrangement of the collection received an adjustment and decoration, that makes it a worthy frame for the Danish Regalia. The walls are hung with costly Oriental carpets, interwoven with gold, which dating from Christian V's time have since been used on the solemnity of the coronation. Over the door, in a frame of ebony, hangs the original escutcheon of Denmark; it is of silver, 16 inches high by 20 broad, and enamelled in its proper colours. The ceiling is a very beautiful work in stucco, and the floor is covered with black and white marble slabs. In the middle of the floor a pyramid arises behind clear thick plate-glass, from the flat sides of which covered with red velvet the rays of gold and precious stones flash upon us, whilst the summit is adorned by a magnificent and costly crown, which was used by the Danish kings after the introduction of absolutism. The objects, preserved here, are:

The ancient Regalia.

On the right side: The state sword of Christian III of gold and richly adorned with enamel and diamonds &c.

The crown of Christian IV; it is open, of gold with chased and embossed work and ornamented by figures in enamel and diamonds: It is in every respect a highly valuable and significant work of art, said to have been executed by the renowned goldsmith Diderik Fiuren in Odense.

The original copy of the lex regia in the hand-writing of its author Peter Schumacher (Griffenfeld) and with the original signature of Frederik III and the royal seal attaches. Further more the silver-case belonging to it, on which is engraved: Lex Regia. Frider. 3. MDCLXV. XIV Novembris.

The new Regalia.

On the top of the pyramid: the latter crown, which in contra distinction to that of Christian IV is with closed curvatures and bears on the summit the cross and globe (which form was first common in the days of the absolute power). It is of gold, set with a multitude of precious stones, of which four are above all of an extraordinary size ane value (two rubies and two sapphires); they are placed in the lowest rim.

On the side towards the drilling ground: the globe, of gold with a band of diamonds, upon a blue enamelled ground, and a cross likewise decorated with diamonds; the sword, with a gold hilt set with diamonds; the sheath adorned with the arms of the kingdom and the provinces in enamel and diamonds; the broad band, to which it is hung, is embroidered in gold and decorated with diamonds and enamel; the sceptre, of gold with diamonds and enamel, terminates in the form of a crowned lily; the box for the consecrating oil, of gold with enamel and diamonds.

These objects, remarkable for their exquisite workmanship, are said to have been executed by the celebrated Casper Herbach (»Art-Casper«) and were used for the first time at the coronation of Christian V Juni 7th 1671.

The large amethyst, which decorates the canopy of the Royal chair upon the day of coronation; it is enamelled underneath and adorned with the monogram of Christian V.

The original order of the elephant with the chain (composed of elephants that are linked together by towers), all of gold and decorated by enamel and diamonds; the star of brilliants belonging to the order; another of eight rays, embroidered with silver-thread and thickly set with pearls. The one last named is ,intended as an ornament for the royal mantle.

The original Dannebroge-order: a white enamelled gold-cross with red edges, set with diamonds. The chain is composed of, alternate, white enamelled gold crosses with red edges, the crowned monogram of Christian V and a crowned W (Valdemar the Victorious). — The insignia of both orders with their belongings are from the time of Christian V.

We further remark: a garter, belonging to the coronation dress of the king.

Upon the side opposite the door: The large royal goblet (to taste from before it is presented to the king on his coronation-day), of pure gold, with embossed, chased and enamelled work, that bears the mark of a great master's hand (upon the cover are six swans who bear the Regalia in their beaks &c.). Executed in Holland in the time of Frederik III. — A dish with a can and a pair of candlesticks of embossed gold, which are used at the Christening of the royal children (from the time of Frederik III). In accordance with an old arrangement it has been the usage to inscribe the full name of the baptized child on the under part of the dish, and this having been done from its first employment until now, it has thus preserved an enduring record of the recurrences of its use.

Upon the left side:

The queens crown of gold with diamonds &c.

The crownjewels, namely, besides some single smaller diamond-ornaments, which retain their original settings, the following ornaments, which in the time of Christian VIII were re-set in more modern taste by the jeweller Weishaupt in Hanau:

1, A neck-lace, consisting of 45 large brilliants with earrings to match.

2, A neck-lace of very large rose-diamonds.

3, A necklace of large pearls; in the middle an ornament of brilliants and rubies. To this belongs a stomacher and earrings, likewise of brilliants, rubies and pearls.

4, A neck-lace of emeralds and brilliants with earrings of the same. To this belongs a diadem and stomacher also of emeralds and brilliants.

5, A large bouquet for the bosom of white and yellow brilliants.

The crown is indebted for the greater part of these jewels to the testamentary dispositions of the queen dowager Sophia Magdalena and the princess Charlotta Amalia, dated respectively Oct. 10th 1746 and July 1st 1773.